High-Interest
READING

by
Walter A. Hazen

Cover Design by
Matthew Van Zomeren

Inside Illustrations by
Don O'Connor

Publisher
Instructional Fair • TS Denison
Grand Rapids, Michigan 49544

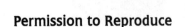

Permission to Reproduce

About the Author

Walter A. Hazen received his Bachelor of Science in Education from Troy State University. He also holds a master's degree from the University of Tennessee, where he specialized in deaf education. A secondary history teacher with over 30 years of experience, Walter spent the last several years of his career teaching and developing curriculum for deaf students.

Credits

Author: Walter A. Hazen
Cover Design: Matthew Van Zomeren
Inside Illustrations: Don O'Connor
Project Director/Editor: Sharon Kirkwood
Editors: Lisa Hancock, Eunice Kuiper
Typesetting/Layout: Pat Geasler

Standard Book Number: 1-56822-614-4
High-Interest Reading
Copyright © 1998 by Instructional Fair • TS Denison
2400 Turner NW
Grand Rapids, Michigan 49544

Table of Contents

Little Sure Shot 4–5

Nerve and Brain Pills 6–7

The Ferocious Piranha 8–9

Emperor Norton 10–11

Laughter: Good Medicine 12–13

Coral, Scarlet, or Scarlet King? 14–15

"Wrong-Way" Corrigan 16–17

"Wrong-Way" Riegels 18–19

The *Mary Celeste* 20–21

One Big Lizard! 22–23

Steel-Driving Man 24–25

The Children's Crusade 26–27

Maternal Fish Fathers 28–29

"An Apple a Day…" 30–31

The Black Death 32–33

The Story of Evangeline 34–35

Dogfights 36–37

The Ship of the Desert 38–39

A True Hero 40–41

One Stubborn Italian! 42–43

Ant Ambushers 44–45

The Littlest Major Leaguer 46–47

Sod Houses 48–49

How Mr. Lincoln Got His Beard 50–51

Atlantis: Real or Imagined? 52–53

"Wilt the Stilt" 54–55

The Ghost Dance 56–57

Joe Magarac 58–59

The Boys in the Breakers 60–61

Black Cowboys 62–63

Championship Sack Racing? 64–65

Stagecoach Mary 66–67

Broadway Joe 68–69

Althea Gibson: Tennis Trailblazer 70–71

Becoming a Better Reader 72

Answer Key (in middle of book)

Little Sure Shot

Would you believe a 15-year-old girl so skilled with a pistol that she could hit a playing card, thin edge out, by shooting backwards over her shoulder? Most people would find that hard to believe, and Frank Butler was no exception.

Frank Butler, renowned sharpshooter, felt confident, and maybe even a little cocky, as he watched his opponent in an arranged shooting match step from a stagecoach in Cincinnati. How could a pretty teenage girl from the backwoods of Ohio possibly pose a challenge to one of the greatest marksmen in America?

Phoebe Ann Moses did more than just pose a challenge to the haughty Butler. She held steady during the shooting contest and won easily. Was Frank Butler impressed? Very. He later married Annie—as she came to call herself.

Annie Oakley was a natural-born shooter. Starting at the age of 9, she shot a walnut off a tree branch the very first time she fired her father's old long-barreled rifle. Her skill with the gun proved a blessing for her family, because her father had died of a fever when she was four. Annie helped support her mother, brothers, and sisters by shooting and selling quail and rabbits.

After she married, Annie and her husband, Frank, joined Buffalo Bill Cody's Wild West Show in 1885. Annie was an immediate sensation and remained so for seventeen years. Her name appeared on billboards throughout America and Europe. She performed for the likes of England's Queen Victoria and once shot a cigarette from the mouth of Kaiser Wilhelm of Germany. She also thrilled crowds by shooting glass objects thrown into the air as she rode by on a galloping horse. Out of a thousand glass targets, Annie could hit 999 of them.

Annie Oakley was five feet tall and weighed only 98 pounds. When she joined the Wild West Show, she was 25, but she looked all of 16. Sweet-faced and dainty, everybody loved "Little Sure Shot," as Annie came to be called.

Place a check (✔) in front of each statement that is true.

Annie Oakley . . .

_____ 1. was nine years old when she beat Frank Butler in a shooting contest.

_____ 2. was born in Cincinnati.

_____ 3. once helped support her family by shooting and selling quail and rabbits.

_____ 4. married Frank Butler.

_____ 5. was tall in stature for a woman.

_____ 6. joined Buffalo Bill Cody's Wild West Show.

_____ 7. could shoot glass objects thrown into the air while riding a galloping horse.

Which words in paragraph #2 mean the same as the words below?

1. well-known (adj)   _____

2. planned (adj)   _____

3. threat (noun)   _____

Nerve and Brain Pills

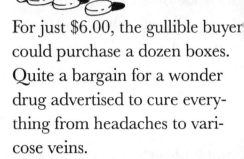

Since time began, people have sought miracle cures for whatever ailed them. Many put their faith in quacks who eagerly accepted their money but left them no better off than before. Many others have spent small fortunes on such cure-alls as Hamlin's Wizard Oil, Reliable Worm Syrup and Worm Cakes, and Dr. B.P. Sherman's Pricklyrash Bitters. None of these "medicines," however, did much to help the desperate patient.

Not all miracle medicines were sold at carnivals or by traveling peddlers. Mail-order catalogs devoted countless pages to advertising such remedies. The author's personal favorite comes straight from the 1902 edition of the Sears, Roebuck Catalog. Called "Dr. Hammond's Nerve and Brain Pills," they were guaranteed to cure a remarkable number of ailments. —and at only 60 cents a box!

For just $6.00, the gullible buyer could purchase a dozen boxes. Quite a bargain for a wonder drug advertised to cure everything from headaches to varicose veins.

Among other physical problems, Dr. Hammond's Brain and Nerve Pills were said to cure blurred vision, lifelessness, chills and hot flushes, and shortness of breath. Also guaranteed to respond favorably were heart palpitations, poor blood circulation, cold feet, indigestion, chest and back pains, and spots before the eyes. But, suppose a person's complaints were of a psychological nature and not physical in any way? No problem—Dr. Hammond's Brain and Nerve Pills had that covered too. Three boxes were considered sufficient to take

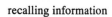

care of anxiety, low spirits, and even poor memory. Even if a person did not suffer from any physical or mental malady, Dr. Hammond's amazing pills could still be of benefit. What about getting rid of excess flabbiness? Dr. Hammond's pills promised to take care of that, too.

To be more convincing, the advertisement warned people to beware of quacks selling useless remedies. It points out that Dr. Hammond's pills had been used successfully in Germany for years.

If buyers were embarrassed to order Dr. Hammond's pills from the Sears, Roebuck catalog, they were assured that their shipment would arrive in a plain sealed wrapper. That way, they could avoid any good-natured ribbing.

Lst any 6 ailments that Dr. Hammond's pills were said to cure.

1. _____   4. _____

2. _____   5. _____

3. _____   6. _____

Answer the questions below.

1. Dr. Hammond's Nerve and Brain Pills were advertised in the 1902 catalog of the _____ Company.

2. Dr. Hammond's Brain and Nerve Pills cost _____ cents a box.

3. For $6.00, a person could buy _____ boxes of the pills.

4. The pills were advertised as having been used successfully in _____ before becoming available in the U.S.

The Ferocious Piranha

People who travel or cross the Amazon and Orinoco Rivers of South America are careful never to dangle a foot or hand from the side of their boat. For just below the surface of these mighty waters lurks a small fish feared throughout the continent. That fish is the flesh-eating piranha. It has a nasty disposition and an even nastier appetite.

The natives of the Amazon and Orinoco regions fear no animal more than the piranha. Not even crocodiles strike greater fear in the local inhabitants. This is due to the fact that the piranha fears nothing. Although smaller fish make up most of its diet, it will attack both humans and other animals, and size is of no consequence. Piranhas have been known to strip every ounce of flesh off a carcass in a matter of minutes.

Two characteristics make piranhas such fearsome predators. First, they have powerful jaws lined with razor-sharp teeth. These teeth enable the small fish to slice off large chunks of a victim's flesh with lightning quickness. So sharp are the piranha's teeth that it's been said that some South American Indians used them to make tips for their arrows.

A second frightening characteristic of piranhas is that they never attack alone. They always go after their victim in schools ranging from one hundred to a thousand. Any splashing or activity in the water immediately attracts their attention, and the smell of blood turns them into frenzied demons.

There are about twenty different kinds of piranhas, and some of them resemble other fish that eat plants and pose no threat to humans. But anyone not skilled at distinguishing between these blood-thirsty cannibals and their harmless cousins had best stay away from the water!

Below are statements from the story about the piranha. To the left of each, write **F** if it is a fragment, or part of a sentence. Write **S** if it is a complete sentence.

____ 1. A small fish that fears nothing.

____ 2. It will attack anything, regardless of size.

____ 3. Teeth as sharp as razors.

____ 4. Attacks in large schools.

____ 5. Natives have much respect for the piranha.

____ 6. The Amazon River is in South America.

____ 7. Piranhas have a nasty disposition.

____ 8. Piranhas will even attack humans.

____ 9. Twenty different kinds of piranhas.

____ 10. Have strong, powerful jaws.

____ 11. Blood-thirsty cannibals.

____ 12. The smell of blood turns them into frenzied demons.

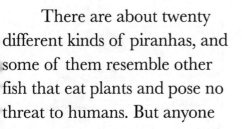

FRONT VIEW
OF SKULL

Emperor Norton

He went about in full military uniform with gold epaulets on his shoulders. He was the center of attention at civic and social gatherings. Most restaurants gladly served him free of charge, and a San Francisco newspaper good-naturedly printed his decrees and proclamations. Who was this royal person from the not-too-well-known pages of American history? None other than Joshua A. Norton, the self-proclaimed Emperor of the United States.

Norton I, as he called himself, was no emperor at all. He was a harmless old gentleman who had once made and lost a fortune in the real estate business. When he went bankrupt shortly before the beginning of the Civil War, his loss apparently affected his mind. He began telling people that the California legislature had appointed him emperor of the entire nation. Everyone in San Francisco went along with the ruse, and for over 25 years, Norton I ruled happily over his subjects.

Norton was born in England in 1819 and emigrated to San Francisco at the age of thirty. Arriving with $40,000, he was soon worth more than six times that amount. But a bad investment resulted in complete financial disaster, and the shaken Englishman withdrew into seclusion. When he emerged after some time, he sent a letter to the *San Francisco Bulletin* "announcing" his appointment as emperor.

Norton I took daily strolls through San Francisco's streets, greeting his subjects and settling minor disputes. To earn money, he issued bonds that citizens kindly bought for fifty cents each. Norton even printed his own money, which most restaurants and even a few banks honored. Everyone in San Francisco seemed to look at the emperor as a form of comic amusement—a welcome relief from the cares of the day. When he passed in the streets, men often bowed and ladies curtsied.

Norton I died in 1881, a happy "monarch" with a loyal following.

Complete the statements below about Emperor Norton.

1. Newspapers published Emperor Norton's proclamations and _____.

2. Norton I printed his own _____.

3. The emperor's military jacket came with _____ on the shoulders.

4. Norton made a fortune in _____ estate.

5. Joshua A. Norton thought he was an _____.

6. Norton arrived in America with the sum of _____ dollars.

7. Emperor Norton was born in _____.

8. The citizens of San Francisco bought _____ issued by Norton I.

9. Norton was _____ years old when he immigrated to America.

10. The *San Francisco* _____ announced Norton's appointment as Emperor of the United States.

Laughter: Good Medicine

"Go home, have yourself a couple of good laughs, and call me in the morning."

Such advice from a doctor to a patient may not be as far-fetched as it sounds. The relationship between laughter and health has long been suspected. As early as the fifteenth century, a surgeon in Europe told jokes to his patients in the belief that laughter sped the recovery process. Several hundred years later, an English educator recommended tickling under the armpits as a way to treat moodiness. On our own continent, medicine men of the Ojibwa tribe thought along those same lines. They did humorous stunts to make patients laugh away their illnesses.

Physically, it is a kind of inner exercise that some scientists believe strenghthens the heart and lungs. It also provides a good workout for the muscles of the chest, stomach, and diaphragm. In addition, laughter burns calories and may actually help lower blood pressure. Some scientists think it can even help relieve the symptoms of headaches, infections, and arthritis.

But by far the greatest benefits of laughter are psychological. You have probably noticed this yourself on days when you are a little "down in the dumps." When nothing seems to lift your mood, a friend appears and tells you a really funny joke. You laugh, and almost immediately you feel better.

Laughter also helps relieve stress and tension. If you are nervous about an upcoming test or some kind of school function, laughter can help you relax and cope better with the situation. Many anxieties and fears are lessened by a simple dose of laughter.

The benefits of laughter to both our physical and mental health have been proven time and again. So, the next time you feel stressed over an exam, roll in the floor, tickle yourself, and have a good laugh.

On the line to the left of each statement, write **F** if you think the statement is a fact. Write **O** if you think it is an opinion.

_____ 1. People who laugh are always happy.

_____ 2. Laughter alone can cure depression.

_____ 3. Scientists have proven that laughter is important to physical and mental well-being.

_____ 4. Laughter can help relieve anxiety and stress.

_____ 5. Laughter can be used to treat all illnesses.

_____ 6. Laughter serves as a kind of inner exercise.

_____ 7. Laughter may someday replace conventional medicine in the treatment of disease.

Answer the questions below.

1. What is the main idea expressed in "Laughter: Good Medicine"?

_____

_____

2. What is the main idea of Paragraph 2?

_____

_____

Coral, Scarlet, or Scarlet King?

If you live in the South or in certain parts of the West, chances are you have encountered a coral snake. Or have you? Could you say with any certainty that what you happened upon was not a scarlet snake or a scarlet king snake?

At first glance, all three of these colorful snakes might look the same to someone unfamiliar with each one. Each has alternating bands of black, red, and yellow. Each measures about 18 inches in length, although the common coral snake of the South may be twice that length. And unlike larger, broader snakes, the coral, scarlet, and scarlet king snakes all have slender bodies.

So, how do you tell them apart? First, the scarlet snake is extremely rare and docile, and is found only in the southeast. It is different from the coral snake and the scarlet king snake in that its colored bands do not encircle its belly. Turn a scarlet snake over and you will find that its underside is yellow.

The poisonous coral snake and the scarlet king snake are more common. But they are just as easy to identify as the scarlet snake. The red bands of the coral snake are always bordered by yellow, while the red bands of the scarlet king snake are bordered by black. But there is a quicker, easier way to distinguish between the two snakes. Look at their snouts or heads. The snout of the scarlet king snake is always red, followed by yellow and black. The snout of the coral snake is always black—for the common coral it's **black**-yellow-black and for the western coral it's **black**-yellow-red.

Although coral snakes are

highly poisonous, few people are bitten by them. They are extremely shy and are seldom seen. The only way to be bitten by a coral snake is to step on it or handle it.

A wise rule to follow regarding snakes is not to pick up *any* of them. Most snakes will bite if bothered, and even a harmless snake can give you a nasty infection.

Although the story you read discusses three snakes, the Venn diagram asks you to compare only the coral and scarlet king snakes, which more closely resemble each other. List features common to both where the circles overlap.

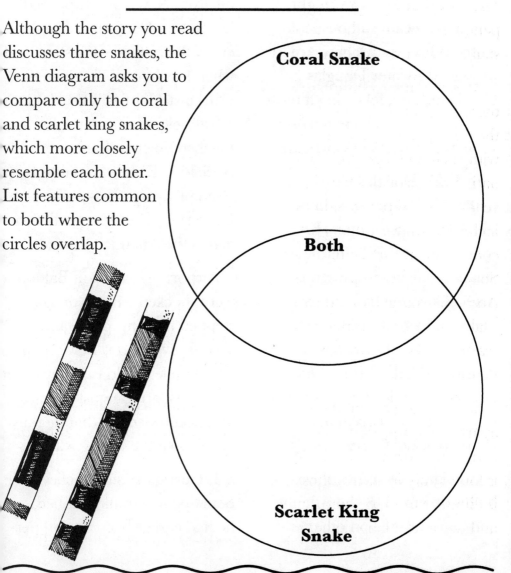

Coral Snake

Both

Scarlet King Snake

"Wrong-Way" Corrigan

He was greeted by enthusiastic crowds in Paris and London. When he returned to the United States, he was given one of the largest ticker-tape parades in New York history. Overnight, his name became a household word. Who was this new American hero? Aviator Douglas Corrigan, who, following a most unusual feat, was known worldwide as Wrong-Way Corrigan.

In 1937, Douglas Corrigan had requested permission to fly the Atlantic to Europe. His request was denied after federal aviation officials inspected his plane. Corrigan had added so many extra gas tanks to his dilapidated craft that it was considered a deathtrap. One tank was even located directly in front of the pilot's seat and nearly blocked Corrigan's vision.

Corrigan apparently gave up on his dream to fly the Atlantic and concentrated on other endeavors. Then, in the predawn hours of July 16, 1938, he took off from New York, supposedly headed for California. Employees at the airfield were surprised when he directed his plane eastward instead of westward. Some twenty-eight hours later, he touched down at Baldonnel Airfield in Dublin, Ireland! Instead of flying cross-country to California, Corrigan had flown across the Atlantic to Europe!

Airport personnel at Baldonnel were shocked when Corrigan stepped from his plane and sheepishly asked if he were in Los Angeles. Told that he was in Ireland, Corrigan just grinned and acknowledged that he must have flown the wrong way.

Is Corrigan's story believeable? Some people think that because he had earlier been denied permission to fly the Atlantic he simply invented his "wrong way" scheme to cover for his having disobeyed aviation authorities.

Whether legitimate or not, Douglas Corrigan's flight made him famous. It is even more remarkable when one considers that his plane had no radio or other safety devices. All Corrigan had in the cockpit when he took off that morning was a Boy Scout compass and several maps he had torn from an atlas. And, oh yes, two chocolate bars!

On the lines below, summarize the story of "Wrong-Way" Corrigan.

_____

_____

_____

_____

Write the letter of the correct answer in the blank.

_____ 1. Wrong-Way Corrigan's first name was . . .
   (a) Donald.   (b) Dugan.   (c) Douglas.

_____ 2. Corrigan made his famous flight in . . .
   (a) 1937.   (b) 1938.   (c) 1939.

_____ 3. After Corrigan crossed the Atlantic, he landed in . . .
   (a) Paris.   (b) London.   (c) Dublin.

_____ 4. When Corrigan returned to the United States, he was greeted by a tickertape parade in . . .
   (a) Los Angeles.   (b) New York.   (c) Chicago.

_____ 5. Corrigan's flight across the Atlantic took a little over . . .
   (a) 28 hours.   (b) 26 hours.   (c) 24 hours.

"Wrong-Way" Riegels

Roy Riegels was another American who won fame for going the wrong way—this time on a football field. His mental blunder, while serving as captain of the University of California's 1929 football team, resulted in the Golden Bears losing that year's Rose Bowl game to Georgia Tech.

Captain Riegels' monumental mistake occurred in the first half of the game. With Georgia Tech in possession on its own 25-yard line, a Golden Tornado (now Yellow Jackets) back fumbled after receiving a hard hit. The alert Riegels scooped up the ball and turned toward the Georgia Tech goal. But then something happened. Riegels became confused, did a complete about-face, and took off for his own goal some 70 yards away.

The 70,000 spectators watching the game could not believe their eyes. Neither could the players on the field. Everyone just stood and stared. By the time any of Riegels' teammates realized that he was speeding the wrong way, the big center had a huge head start on his pursuers. Sprinting like a runaway locomotive, he was finally pulled down on his own 6-inch line by teammate Benny Lom.

California boosters breathed a sigh of relief. Surely a spiraling, Golden Bear punt from their end zone would push Georgia Tech far enough back to avert disaster. But after Riegels snapped the ball back to Lom, a Golden Tornado lineman broke through and blocked the punt. California recovered the ball, but Georgia Tech was awarded a safety, making the score 2-0 in the Golden Tornadoes' favor.

The shaken Riegels was comforted by his teammates on the sidelines. He was so upset that he almost did not return to the field for the second half. He played, and played admirably, but the damage had been done. Georgia Tech scored a touchdown to go up 8-0, and even though California scored late to reduce the margin to 8-7, the safety that resulted from Riegels' mistake proved to be the margin of victory.

Players in other sports have made similar mental errors that led to defeats just as agonizing. But life goes on, and once the pain heals and the game is forgotten, the great athletes recover to play again.

Number the following events in the order in which they occurred.

____ Georgia Tech is awarded a safety.

____ Roy Riegels scoops up a Tech fumble.

____ Riegels snaps the ball to punter Benny Lom.

____ The Rose Bowl game begins.

____ California scores a late touchdown.

____ Georgia Tech fumbles on its own 25-yard line.

____ Lom tackles Riegels on the California 6-inch line.

____ Georgia Tech block's Benny Lom's punt.

____ Riegels begins running toward his own goal.

____ Teammates take off in pursuit of Riegels.

____ Teammates comfort Riegels on the sideline following his mistake.

The *Mary Celeste*

The history of the sea is rife with strange stories of derelicts, or ships abandoned by their crew. And none is stranger than the story of the *Mary Celeste*.

The *Mary Celeste,* an American ship, was sighted adrift near the Azores in December 1872. Sailors sent from a British ship to investigate the derelict were surprised at what they found. Except for a tattered sail, everything aboard the *Mary Celeste* appeared normal. Her cargo of barrels of alcohol was undisturbed. Nowhere were there signs of a struggle. The only hint of a disaster were clothes scattered about in the ship's living quarters. Whatever had happened, the ship's occupants had seemingly left in a hurry.

The log of the *Mary Celeste* revealed that she had set sail from New York a month earlier, bound for Genoa, Italy, with her cargo of alcohol. The ship's captain apparently had no reason to expect anything but a routine voyage, for he had taken along his wife and two-year-old daughter. But something did happen, and old sailors for years afterwards gathered at inns to trade stories of mutiny and murder.

Sea historians say nothing of the sort happened. Most researchers believe that the crew and passengers abandoned the *Mary Celeste* after a leak was discovered in the barrels of alcohol. The ship had encountered a storm a few days before, and rough seas could have caused the barrels to bang together and result in explosive fumes escaping throughout the vessel. Fear of an explosion might have resulted in the captain's ordering all hands into the ship's lifeboat to wait at a safe distance for whatever might occur. The researchers think the lifeboat may have been tied to the ship by a long towline.

What happened after that is anybody's guess. Some people think the lifeboat capsized and all its occupants drowned. Others believe that the towline con- necting the lifeboat to the *Mary Celeste* broke. If this is true, the *Mary Celeste* then sailed away of its own accord, leaving its former passengers to die a slow death from hunger and the elements.

Choose a word from the Word Bank to complete each sentence.

Word	believe	escaping	disaster	certain	fate
Bank	derelict	carrying	expected	drowned	seemed

1. The *Mary Celeste* was a famous _____.

2. No one knows for _____ what happened to the *Mary Celeste*.

3. The *Mary Celeste* was _____ a cargo of alcohol.

4. The ship's captain had _____ a routine voyage.

5. Somewhere near the Azores, _____ struck the *Mary Celeste*.

6. Everything _____ in order aboard the abandoned ship.

7. Researchers think _____ fumes might have caused the crew and passengers to leave the ship.

8. The _____ of the crew and passengers may never be fully determined.

9. Some researchers think the people in the lifeboat _____.

10. Other people _____ the towline connecting the life boat with the *Mary Celeste* broke.

One Big Lizard!

Some lizards are cute little reptiles no more than a few centimeters in length. Some you can pick up and perhaps even take home for pets. But would you believe a lizard exists that can grow to be 10 feet long and weigh 300 pounds? Now, *that's* a lizard!

The so-called Komodo dragon is the largest lizard in the world. It lives on several islands in Indonesia. It belongs to a group of lizards called "monitors," because according to legend they warn of the presence of crocodiles.

The Komodo somewhat resembles the fire-breathing dragons of myth and legend. That is how it came to be called "dragon." Like all monitors, the Komodo has a long, forked tongue that retracts into a sheath like a sword. Both its head and neck are long, and it has powerful legs that make it a swift runner on land. Its red mouth is lined with rows of sharp teeth that enable it to eat small animals.

Unlike smaller lizards that live on insects and plants, the Komodo dragon is carnivorous. That means it eats only meat. Although it includes carrion, or dead animals, in its diet, it also chases down and eats goats, deer and wild pigs. Its ability to catch swift animals such as deer and goats is indicative of its speed.

The Komodo dragon is also a good swimmer, moving along in the water much like a crocodile or alligator. Holding its legs against its sides, it drives itself forward by wriggling its body and long tail.

The origin of the Komodo dragon is shrouded in mystery. Scientists do not know for certain where it came from, and it inhabits only a few islands in Indonesia. It has been known and studied by the Western world for less than a century. Why it grew to such an enormous size is also a mystery. Some scientists think that the absence of any predator of competitive size may have resulted in the lizard evolving into the giant it is.

Read each of the following statements. Write **T** if the statement is true or **F** if it is false.

___ 1. The Komodo dragon is the largest lizard in the world.

___ 2. The Komodo dragon is a true, fire-breathing dragon.

___ 3. Dragons once existed throughout the world.

___ 4. The Komodo dragon is one kind of monitor lizard.

___ 5. Monitor lizards are so-called because it was once believed they gave warning when crocodiles were nearby.

___ 6. The Komodo dragon lives throughout southeast Asia.

___ 7. Komodo dragons eat only meat.

___ 8. A Komodo dragon swims by moving its short, powerful legs.

___ 9. A Komodo dragon can chase down a goat or deer.

___ 10. Some Komodo dragons are found in the Western Hemisphere.

___ 11. Scientists think the Komodo dragon may have come from China.

___ 12. The Komodo dragon eats only live animals.

Steel-Driving Man

For more than a century, Americans have sung about the mighty deeds of John Henry. You have probably heard the ballad, or folk song, about this giant among railroad workers. The song tells the story of a "steel-driving man" who competed in a contest with a steam drill.

There really was a person named John Henry. He was an African-American railroad construction worker. But according to most accounts, he died from an accident in a railroad tunnel. Writers generally contend that the race against the steam drill is invented folklore.

Lovers of legends and folk tales, however, think otherwise. They believe that the duel with the steam drill actually occurred. Some say it took place in West Virginia in 1870. Others maintain that it happened in Alabama about the year 1882.

One version of the story relates how John Henry could drive steel ten hours at a stretch without stopping. Crowds would gather to watch as he hammered holes in rocks in which explosive were placed. This was the manner used to blast away rock to construct railroad tunnels.

One day at John Henry's work site, a salesman appeared peddling a "newfangled" machine. The machine was the steam drill. The salesman boasted that it could drill holes in rock many times faster than a man. When John Henry saw that his boss wa impressed, he proposed a wager. He bet that he could drive a deeper hole than the machine—and in less time.

The race was on. With a 20-pound hammer in each hand, John Henry pounded away. The steam drill bored and grunted.

Spectators who had gathered for the event screamed and cheered. After a half-hour, John Henry had drilled two seven-foot holes. The steam drill had bored one hole nine-feet deep. The mighty railroad worker was clearly the winner.

John Henry became the workingman's hero. His contest with the steam drill came to symbolize the worker's struggle against the coming of machines. A new Industrial Revolution that began in the late nineteenth century caused workers everywhere to fear the loss of their jobs.

With each word listed below, underline the meaning which best defines the word as it is used in the story.

1. **drive**: direct by a blow or thrust; make go; to guide and control an automobile

2. **deed**: written statement of ownership; act or feat; a document

3. **contend**: compete; struggle; declare to be a fact

4. **legend**: an explanation of symbols on a map; inscription on a coin or medal; a story handed down from the past

5. **stretch**: a continuous period of time; to make longer or wider; a term of imprisonment

6. **propose**: make an offer of marriage; suggest; intend or plan

7. **revolution**: the overthrow of a government; a movement in a circle around some point; a complete change

8. **drill**: training and instruction; a tool or machine for making holes; a practice lesson

The Children's Crusade

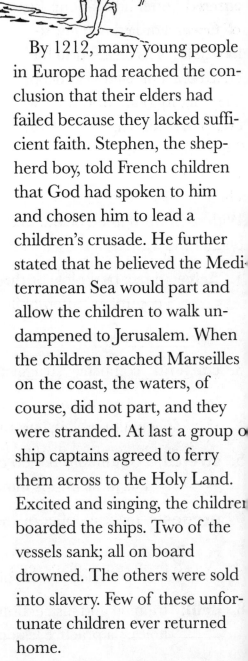

In the year 1212, two armies of children no older than their early teens departed Europe on an unusual mission. One group of 20,000, led by a 12-year-old shepherd boy named Stephen, left France. Another group of 30,000, under the leadership of a lad named Nicholas, left Germany. Where were these youngsters going? To the Holy Land—the birthplace of Jesus—to free it from the control of the Muslims. And they were going without weapons!

Near the end of the eleventh century, Israel, or the Holy Land, was taken over by the Muslim Turks. Almost immediately, Christian knights set out from Europe determined to throw out the Turks. In a series of military expeditions that continued for 200 years, the Christian armies were never able to regain permanent control of the area. These expeditions to the Holy Land are referred to as the Crusades.

By 1212, many young people in Europe had reached the conclusion that their elders had failed because they lacked sufficient faith. Stephen, the shepherd boy, told French children that God had spoken to him and chosen him to lead a children's crusade. He further stated that he believed the Mediterranean Sea would part and allow the children to walk undampened to Jerusalem. When the children reached Marseilles on the coast, the waters, of course, did not part, and they were stranded. At last a group of ship captains agreed to ferry them across to the Holy Land. Excited and singing, the children boarded the ships. Two of the vessels sank; all on board drowned. The others were sold into slavery. Few of these unfortunate children ever returned home.

Nicholas and his following of German youngsters met a fate almost as bad. Leaving the city of Cologne, they were determined to cross the Alps to the Italian port of Genoa. There they hoped to obtain ships to complete their trip to the Holy Land. But on the journey across the mountains, many of the children died of hunger or were killed by wild animals. Those who made it to Genoa were ridiculed by Italian sailors, who refused to take them across the sea. The children appealed to the pope for help, but he kindly told them to go home. Disheartened, some struggled back across the Alps to Germany while others stayed on in Genoa.

Answers the questions below.

1. What do events such as the Children's Crusade tell us about life in the Middle Ages?

_____

_____

2. Why do you think Christian Europe was upset when the Muslim Turks gained control of the Holy Land?

_____

_____

3. Why do you think the parents allowed their children to go?

_____

_____

Maternal Fish Fathers

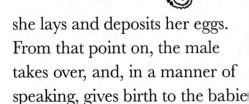

In the warm and temperate waters of the world live two most unusual fish: the seahorse and its relative, the pipefish.

The seahorse, so-called because its head resembles that of a horse, is a small fish about 2 to 8 inches long. It swims in a vertical position by moving the dorsal fin on its back. It is the only fish with a prehensile tail that it uses, like a monkey, to coil around and cling to seaweed.

The pipefish is named for its long snout, which resembles a narrow pipe. When its body is straight, the pipefish resembles a slender snake. It too moves along in an upright position. Its body forms an *S* shape and is propelled by its rear fins.

But it is not appearance that makes the seahorse and the pipefish unique. It is their reproductive habits. With both fish, the female's responsibility in the reproductive process ends when she lays and deposits her eggs. From that point on, the male takes over, and, in a manner of speaking, gives birth to the babie

Both the male seahorse and the male pipefish have pouch-like organs on their undersides in which the female deposits her eggs. Here the young fish stay an nourish for a gestation period of either a few days or several week depending on the species. When the baby seahorses are ready to be born, the father seahorse attaches itself to a plant and actually goes through the pangs of childbirth. As it bends back and forth, the wall of its brood pouch contracts, and with each spasm, a baby fish is introduced to the world of the sea. The birtl of the baby pipefish is less dramatic. The father's pouch simply opens and the offspring swim of on their own.

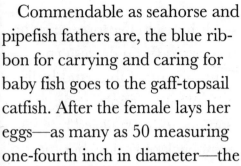

Commendable as seahorse and pipefish fathers are, the blue ribbon for carrying and caring for baby fish goes to the gaff-topsail catfish. After the female lays her eggs—as many as 50 measuring one-fourth inch in diameter—the male scoops them up and carries them in his mouth for a period of eighty days. During this entire time, while the babies are living off their own yolk, the father catfish does not eat.

Write **T** if the statement is true and **F** if it is false.

_____ 1. The seahorse's name comes from its peculiar movement.

_____ 2. The pipefish swims by using fins situated near its head.

_____ 3. The seahorse swims in an upright position.

_____ 4. The snout of the pipefish closely resembles a smoker's pipe.

_____ 5. The seahorse is the only fish equipped with a grasping tail.

_____ 6. The pipefish is unable to swim in a vertical position.

_____ 7. Both the female seahorse and the female pipefish help care for their babies after they are born.

_____ 8. Female seahorses and pipefish deposit their eggs in their mates' pouches.

_____ 9. Male seahorses actually go through the pangs of childbirth.

_____ 10. Pipefish are all born at once when their father's pouch opens.

_____ 11. The female gaff-topsail catfish lays about fifty eggs at a time.

_____ 12. The male gaff-topsail catfish carries the female's eggs in his mouth.

"An Apple a Day..."

If you enjoy a nice, juicy apple as do most people, you should find the story of Johnny Appleseed interesting.

Johnny Appleseed's real name was John Chapman. He was born in Massachusetts in 1774. In the early 1800s, he moved to western Pennsylvania, and it is here that his story really begins.

Johnny became widely known as a combination nurseryman, herb doctor, and storyteller. He also served in the War of 1812 as a messenger. Johnny was deeply religious and believed it was his calling to plant apple trees throughout the Ohio Valley. He was very popular with frontier people, who saw him as a true friend and something of a religious prophet.

As settlers passed through the Ohio Valley on their way west, he gave or sold them apple seeds and saplings. Later, he followed their paths, caring for mature trees and planting more seeds himself. For forty years he wandered through western Pennsylvania, Ohio, and Indiana, planting apple seeds. Sometimes he traveled by horseback or canoe, but most of the time he walked. Native Americans never bothered him; they respected him because of his ability to endure hardships and suffering.

Johnny traveled through the forests barefoot and clad in rags. He slept in the open in freezing weather without shoes or any kind of coat. Even when he stopped at a frontier cabin for the night, he usually ate and slept outside. The last thing he did before falling asleep was read from his Bible.

Every year Johnny returned home for more seeds. These he obtained from the cider mills of western Pennsylvania. After filling his sacks with as many seeds as they would hold, he would set out again for Ohio.

Johnny always went out of his way to be kind to animals. People who knew him said he was reluctant to kill even a mosquito. Once he rescued a wolf from a trap, and the grateful animal became his pet. It followed him on his travels.

One might think that Johnny would have "retired" from planting apple seeds after a number of years. But he never did. At the age of 72, he died peacefully one night outside a settler's cabin. He was still carrying out his life's mission.

Write the letter of the correct answer in the blank.

_____ 1. Johnny Appleseed's real surname (last name) was . . .
    (a) Cheatham.   (b) Chapman.
    (c) Chaplin.   (d) Cappleman.

_____ 2. Johnny Appleseed was born in . . .
    (a) Pennsylvania. (b) Ohio.
    (c) Massachusetts. (d) New York.

_____ 3. Johnny served in the . . .
    (a) Revolutionary War. (b) French and Indian War.
    (c) War of 1812.   (d) Civil War.

_____ 4. Johhny traveled mostly by . . .
    (a) foot.   (b) horseback.
    (c) canoe.   (d) raft.

_____ 5. With regard to Johnny Appleseed, the Indians . . .
    (a) feared him.   (b) respected him.
    (c) hated him.   (d) had no opinion whatever of him.

_____ 6. The last thing Johnny did before retiring each night was . . .
    (a) whittle toys for children. (b) help settlers wash dishes.
    (c) count his apple seeds.   (d) read from his Bible.

The Black Death

The mid-1300s were terrible years in Europe. Floods had caused widespread famine and the Hundred Years' War between France and England was just beginning. Both of these events would eventually cause thousands of deaths.

Terrible as they were, famine and war could not compare with another disaster that occurred then. That disaster was an epidemic of bubonic plague, or the Black Death. The Black Death was a disease caused by a bacteria. It began in Asia and was carried to Europe by fleas living in the fur of rats aboard ships. It was called the "Black Death" because one of its early signs was black splotches that appeared beneath the skin.

The Black Death first surfaced in Europe in 1347. It started at a place called Kaffa on the Black Sea in southern Russia. A Mongol army that had besieged the city for a year was suddenly stricken with the strange disease. Soldiers of the Mongol army quickly died. In an attempt to infect the defenders of Kaffa, the Mongol commander hurled the bodies of his dead soldiers over the city walls. But most of the town's inhabitants were already infected and dying as quickly as their enemies on the outside. A few survivors sailed to ports in Italy, unknowlingly carrying the terrible disease with them. From Italy, the plague spread across Europe. In just three years, it reached the Scandinavian countries and even Iceland and Greenland. By 1350, about a third of the population of Europe had died from the plague. Some historians say that the Black Death, coupled with famine and war, killed one-half of Europe's population in the fourteenth century.

The Black Death created panic wherever it appeared. At the time, no one knew what caused it, nor did they have any idea how to prevent or treat it. People who went to bed healthy might be dead the following morning. Few patients survived beyond five days. Terror-stricken townsfolk quit jobs, abandoned houses, and fled to the countryside in hopes of avoiding the dread disease.

To this day, the disease has not been eliminated, but when an outbreak occurs somewhere in the world, it can quickly be brought under control. Antibiotics are used to treat those infected with the bacteria.

Answer the questions below.

1. As the Black Death spread from city to city, panic-stricken people fled to the countryside. How might this have been an effective way of avoiding the disease? _____

_____

2. You have learned that the Mongol commander at Kaffa threw the bodies of his soldiers who had died of the plague over the city's walls. Why do you suppose he and a few others did not contract the disease? _____

_____

4. People today hire exterminators to rid their homes and property of pests such as fleas and rats. Is this necessary if the plague, for the most part, is no longer a threat?

_____

_____

The Story of Evangeline

Most people are familiar with Henry Wadsworth Longfellow's poem *Evangeline*. It tells the unhappy story of two young people whose engagement is broken off by war.

The young French girl whom Longfellow called Evangeline in his poem really existed. Her name was Emmeline Labiche. She lived in Acadia, part of the French colony of Nova Scotia in what is now Canada. She grew up in the little village of St. Gabriel. Longfellow in his story called the village Grand-Pré. He called Evangeline's fiance Gabriel, but his real name was Louis Arceneaux.

Just as in Longfellow's poem, Acadia came under the control of the British in the eighteenth century. Later, during the French and Indian War, the Acadians sided with the French against the British. King George II of England accused them of inciting the Indians to attack British troops. As punishment, the village of St. Gabriel (Grand Pré) was burned to the ground and all its inhabitants were exiled.

Emmeline Labiche and her mother were put on a boat and sent to Maryland. Louis Arceneaux was sent to Louisiana. In Longfellow's poem, Evangeline spent the remainder of her life searching for her sweetheart. She wandered from Maryland to Louisiana and even on to the Great Plains. She finally found Gabriel many years later in a poorhouse in Philadelphia. He was an old man dying of a terrible disease. The poem ends with Gabriel dying in Evangeline's arms, and she herself dying soon afterward.

Facts indicate that the story ended differently. Emmeline, or Evangeline, found Louis, or Gabriel, in Louisana. He explained that, having thought he dead, he was now engaged to another girl. The news was too much for Emmeline. Devastated, she was reported to have died hopelessly insane.

The descendants of the Acadians who were sent to Lousiana still live there. They are known as Cajuns and speak a French dialect along with English. They have retained many of the customs and traditions that date back to their early years in Canada.

Number the events in the order in which they appear in the article.

_____ The Acadians are exiled.

_____ Evangeline wanders across the country searching for Gabriel.

_____ Evangeline and Gabriel fall in love.

_____ Gabriel dies in Evangeline's arms.

_____ King George II accuses the Acadians of stirring up the Indians.

_____ Evangeline finds Gabriel in a poorhouse in Philadelphia.

_____ The British burn Grand-Pré to the ground.

Identify the proper names below.

1. Louis Arceneaux _____

2. St. Gabriel _____

3. Cajuns _____

4. Acadia _____

5. Henry Wadsworth Longfellow _____

6. George II _____

Dogfights

From the above title, one might assume that the following story has something to do with fights that were once staged with certain breeds of dogs.

Not true. "Dogfight," in the military sense, refers to those air battles that took place between dashing young pilots in World War I. They started out as simple, almost harmless—and often comical—acts of aggression that eventually turned into deadly bouts of aerial combat. But no one suspected at the war's outset that air battles between enemy planes would even happen at all.

When World War I started, the airplane was little more than 11 years old. Still in its infancy, it was viewed as something of a novelty. Stunt pilots thrilled crowds with crazy antics and acrobatics, but no one in those early years took flight seriously. Most military experts, in fact, saw no future in the airplane. Some even complained that the "flying birdcages" frightened their horses!

At first during the war, the airplane was seen only as a reconnaissance tool. Pilots flew over enemy lines to take photographs and check on troop movement. Little thought was given to harming one another. In fact, when enemy pilots passed in the air, they waved and smiled and then went about their business of scouting and taking pictures.

But then it happened. Perhaps pilots passing in the skies began to shout insults at each other. Or maybe trading snarling glances in passing was enough to do it. Whatever the cause, the days of the friendly skies came to an end. One day an obviously disgruntled pilot took a sack of bricks with him in the air. When an enemy plane passed, he hurled a brick

Answer Key

High-Interest Reading—Grade 6

Page 5

Place a check (✔) in front of each statement that is true.

Annie Oakley . . .

_____ 1. was nine years old when she beat Frank Butler in a shooting contest.

_____ 2. was born in Cincinnati.

✔ 3. once helped support her family by shooting and selling quail and rabbits.

✔ 4. married Frank Butler.

_____ 5. was tall in stature for a woman.

✔ 6. joined Buffalo Bill Cody's Wild West Show.

✔ 7. could shoot glass objects thrown into the air while riding a galloping horse.

Which words in paragraph #2 mean the same as the words below?

1. well-known (adj)   *renowned*

2. planned (adj)   *arranged*

3. threat (noun)   *challenge*

Page 7

Suggested answers:

List any 6 ailments that Dr. Hammond's pills were said to cure.

1. *cold feet*   4. *chest + back pain*

2. *poor circulation*   5. *indigestion*

3. *shortness of breath*   6. *blurred vision*

Answer the questions below.

1. Dr. Hammond's Nerve and Brain Pills were advertised in the 1902 catalog of the *Sears, Roebuck* Company.

2. Dr. Hammond's Brain and Nerve Pills cost *60* cents a box.

3. For $6.00, a person could buy *12* boxes of the pills.

4. The pills were advertised as having been used successfully in *Germany* before becoming available in the U.S.

Page 9

Below are statements from the story about the piranha. To the left of each, write **F** if it is a fragment, or part of a sentence. Write **S** if it is a complete sentence.

F 1. A small fish that fears nothing.

S 2. It will attack anything, regardless of size.

F 3. Teeth as sharp as razors.

F 4. Attacks in large schools.

S 5. Natives have much respect for the piranha.

S 6. The Amazon River is in South America.

S 7. Piranhas have a nasty disposition.

S 8. Piranhas will even attack humans.

F 9. Twenty different kinds of piranhas.

F 10. Have strong, powerful jaws.

E 11. Blood-thirsty cannibals.

S 12. The smell of blood turns them into frenzied demons.

FRONT VIEW OF SKULL

Page 11

Complete the statements below about Emperor Norton.

1. Newspapers published Emperor Norton's proclamations and *decrees*

2. Norton I printed his own *money*.

3. The emperor's military jacket came with *epaulets* on the shoulders.

4. Norton made a fortune in *real* estate.

5. Joshua A. Norton thought he was an *emperor*

6. Norton arrived in America with the sum of *40,000* dollars.

7. Emperor Norton was born in *England*

8. The citizens of San Francisco bought *bonds* issued by Norton I.

9. Norton was *30* years old when he immigrated to America.

10. The *San Francisco Bulletin* announced Norton's appointment as Emperor of the United States.

Page 13

On the line to the left of each statement, write **F** if you think the statement is a fact. Write **O** if you think it is an opinion.

O 1. People who laugh are always happy.

O 2. Laughter alone can cure depression.

F 3. Scientists have proven that laughter is important to physical and mental well-being.

F 4. Laughter can help relieve anxiety and stress.

O 5. Laughter can be used to treat all illnesses.

F 6. Laughter serves as a kind of inner exercise.

O 7. Laughter may someday replace conventional medicine in the treatment of disease.

Answer the questions below.

1. What is the main idea expressed in "Laughter: Good Medicine"?

   Laughter can help improve both physical and mental health.

2. What is the main idea of Paragraph 2?

   Relationship between laughter and health has been known a long time.

Page 15

Coral Snake
1. red bands bordered by yellow or white
2. snouts are black
3. highly poisonous

Both
1. alternating bands of black, red, or yellow
2. measure about 18 inches in length
3. have slender bodies

Scarlet King Snake
1. red bands are bordered by black
2. snout is red
3. nonpoisonous

Page 17

Summaries will vary.

1. c   2. b   3. c   4. b   5. a

Page 19

Number the following events in the order in which they occurred.

9 Georgia Tech is awarded a safety.

3 Roy Riegels scoops up a Tech fumble.

7 Riegels snaps the ball to punter Benny Lom.

1 The Rose Bowl game begins.

11 California scores a late touchdown.

2 Georgia Tech fumbles on its own 25-yard line.

6 Lom tackles Riegels on the California 6-inch line.

8 Georgia Tech block's Benny Lom's punt.

4 Riegels begins running toward his own goal.

5 Teammates take off in pursuit of Riegels.

10 Teammates comfort Riegels on the sideline following his mistake.

Page 21

1. The *Mary Celeste* was a famous **derelict**.
2. No one knows for **certain** what happened to the *Mary Celeste*.
3. The *Mary Celeste* was **carrying** a cargo of alcohol.
4. The ship's captain had **expected** a routine voyage.
5. Somewhere near the Azores, **disaster** struck the *Mary Celeste*.
6. Everything **seemed** in order aboard the abandoned ship.
7. Researchers think **escaping** fumes might have caused the crew and passengers to leave the ship.
8. The **fate** of the crew and passengers may never be fully determined.
9. Some researchers think the people in the lifeboat **drowned**.
10. Other people **believe** the towline connecting the life boat with the *Mary Celeste* broke.

Page 23

Read each of the following statements. Write **T** if the statement is true or **F** if it is false.

T 1. The Komodo dragon is the largest lizard in the world.

F 2. The Komodo dragon is a true, fire-breathing dragon.

F 3. Dragons once existed throughout the world.

T 4. The Komodo dragon is one kind of monitor lizard.

T 5. Monitor lizards are so-called because it was once believed they gave warning when crocodiles were nearby.

F 6. The Komodo dragon lives throughout southeast Asia.

T 7. Komodo dragons eat only meat.

F 8. A Komodo dragon swims by moving its short, powerful legs.

T 9. A Komodo dragon can chase down a goat or deer.

F 10. Some Komodo dragons are found in the Western Hemisphere.

F 11. Scientists think the Komodo dragon may have come from China.

F 12. The Komodo dragon eats only live animals.

Page 25

With each word listed below, underline the meaning which best defines the word as it is used in the story.

1. **drive**: direct by a blow or thrust; make go; to guide and control an automobile

2. **deed**: written statement of ownership; act or feat; a document

3. **contend**: compete; struggle; declare to be a fact

4. **legend**: an explanation of symbols on a map; inscription on a coin or medal; a story handed down from the past

5. **stretch**: a continuous period of time; to make longer or wider; a term of imprisonment

6. **propose**: make an offer of marriage; suggest; intend or plan

7. **revolution**: the overthrow of a government; a movement in a circle around some point; a complete change

8. **drill**: training and instruction; a tool or machine for making holes; a practice lesson

Page 27

Answers the questions below.

1. What do events such as the Children's Crusade tell us about life in the Middle Ages?

   *Religion was very impor-
   tant during the Middle Ages.*

2. Why do you think Christian Europe was upset when the Moslem Turks gained control of the Holy Land?

   *Palestine (the Holy Land) was
   where Jesus was born.*

3. Why do you think the parents allowed their children to go?

   Answers will vary.

Page 29

Write **T** if the statement is true and **F** if it is false.

F 1. The seahorse's name comes from its peculiar movement.

F 2. The pipefish swims by using fins situated near its head.

T 3. The seahorse swims in an upright position.

F 4. The snout of the pipefish closely resembles a smoker's pipe.

T 5. The seahorse is the only fish equipped with a grasping tail.

F 6. The pipefish is unable to swim in a vertical position.

F 7. Both the female seahorse and the female pipefish help care for their babies after they are born.

T 8. Female seahorses and pipefish deposit their eggs in their mates' pouches.

T 9. Male seahorses actually go through the pangs of childbirth.

T 10. Pipefish are all born at once when their father's pouch opens.

T 11. The female gaff-topsail catfish lays about fifty eggs at a time.

T 12. The male gaff-topsail catfish carries the female's eggs in his mouth.

Instructional Fair • TS Denison

IF0304 *High-Interest Reading*

Page 31

Write the letter of the correct answer in the blank.

b 1. Johnny Appleseed's real surname (last name) was . . .
    (a) Cheatham.   (b) Chapman.
    (c) Chaplin.   (d) Cappleman.

c 2. Johnny Appleseed was born in . . .
    (a) Pennsylvania.   (b) Ohio.
    (c) Massachusetts. (d) New York.

c 3. Johnny served in the . . .
    (a) Revolutionary War. (b) French and Indian War.
    (c) War of 1812.   (d) Civil War.

a 4. Johhny traveled mostly by . . .
    (a) foot.   (b) horseback.
    (c) canoe.   (d) raft.

b 5. With regard to Johnny Appleseed, the Indians . . .
    (a) feared him.   (b) respected him.
    (c) hated him.   (d) had no opinion whatever of him.

d 6. The last thing Johnny did before retiring each night was . . .
    (a) whittle toys for children. (b) help settlers wash dishes.
    (c) count his apple seeds. (d) read from his Bible.

Page 33

Answer the questions below.

1. As the Black Death spread from city to city, panic-stricken people fled to the countryside. How might this have been an effective way of avoiding the disease? _Suggested answer: ...by isolating themselves from crowds._

2. You have learned that the Mongol commander at Kaffa threw the bodies of his soldiers who had died of the plague over the city's walls. Why do you suppose he and a few others did not contract the disease? _Some people managed to resist infection_

4. People today hire exterminators to rid their homes and property of pests such as fleas and rats. Is this necessary if the plague, for the most part, is no longer a threat? _Rats and fleas carry many other diseases._

Page 35

Number the events in the order in which they appear in the article.

_4_ The Acadians are exiled.
_5_ Evangeline wanders across the country searching for Gabriel.
_1_ Evangeline and Gabriel fall in love.
_7_ Gabriel dies in Evangeline's arms.
_2_ King George II accuses the Acadians of stirring up the Indians.
_6_ Evangeline finds Gabriel in a poorhouse in Philadelphia.
_3_ The British burn Grand-Pré to the ground.

Identify the proper names below.

1. Louis Arceneaux _Emmeline Labiche's fiance_
2. St. Gabriel _village of Grand-Pré_
3. Cajuns _descendants of Acadians_
4. Acadia _part of Nova Scotia where Evangeline lived_
5. Henry Wadsworth Longfellow _author of Evangeline_
6. George II _English king_

Page 37

On the blank lines below, replace the underlined words with words that make each sentence a true statement.

1. In the story, the term _dogfight_ refers to fights between trained dogs. _air battles during World War I_

2. Most military experts were excited about the future of the airplane in combat. _saw no future for the airplane_

3. At the start of WWI, the airplane was used only for bombing. _reconnaisance_

4. Rusty chains were the first weapons used by pilots in combat. _bricks_

5. Machineguns that fired through an airplane's cockpit made air combat deadly. _propeller blades_

Page 39

Answer the questions below.

1. What is the main idea expressed in the story?
   importance of camel to nomads

2. How are the dromedary and the Bactrian camel different?
   Dromedary has one hump
   Bactrian has two humps

3. What is the purpose of the camel's hump?
   place where camel stores food
   reserves

4. List the physical characteristics that make the camel suitable for desert travel? *Can travel distances without water*
   closes nostril in sandstorm; overhanging
   lid, long lashes shield eyes; padded feet
   don't sink in
   sand

5. Name three ways in which the camel is useful to desert people.
   transportation and portage;
   milk and meat part of nomad's diet;
   sniffs out water holes; hair used for
   tents

Page 41

Write **F** if you think the statement is a fact and **O** if it is an opinion.

O 1. Clemente was the greatest player in the history of baseball.

F 2. Clemente had a lifetime batting average of over .300.

O 3. Had it not been for Clemente, the Pittsburgh Pirates might never have won a National League championship.

O 4. Roberto Clemente was the greatest hitter of all time.

F 5. Clemente helped the Pirates win two World Series championships.

O 6. Had he not died in a tragic accident, Roberto Clemente would have set even more records in baseball.

F 7. Clemente played his entire major league career with the Pittsburgh Pirates.

F 8. Clemente appealed to the people of Puerto Rico to help the victims of the Nicaraguan earthquake.

O 9. All Puerto Ricans loved and respected Roberto Clemente.

O 10. Pilot error probably caused the crash of the DC-7 that killed Clemente and others.

Page 43
1. a   2. b   3. d   4. c   5. d

Page 45

Tiger Beetle
   1. has hooks on its back enabling it to cling to the top of its burrow
   2. uses somersault motion to catch prey
   3. larva lives on as a mature beetle

Both
   1. eat ants and other insects
   2. dig tunnels to trap their prey
   3. live in sandy places such as dunes and deserts

Ant Lion
   1. covers tunnel with layer of sand, causing insects to tumble in
   2. larva changes into an insect resembling a damselfly
   3. adult lives only long enough to mate and lay eggs

Page 47

Answer the questions below.

1. What event was being celebrated on the day Eddie Gaedel appeared in a major league game? *50th Anniversary of American League*

2. What was Sportsman's Park? *St. Louis' ball park*

3. Who were the Browns' opponents in the doubleheader?
   Detroit Tigers

4. What was Eddie told not to do when he stepped up to the plate?
   swing at the ball

5. In your opinion, was it fair or ethical for Browns' owner Bill Veeck to use Eddie in such a way? Was it degrading for Eddie?
   Answers will vary.

6. If you had been Eddie Gaedel, would you have accepted Bill Veeck's invitation to become a part of the entertainment that day? Why or why not? *Answers will vary.*

Page 49

Use the words from the Word Bank to fill in the blanks below.

Word Bank			
boredom	earth	materials	scarce
built	exciting	more	settled
drop	liven	prairie	unexpected

Because other **materials** were **scarce**, pioneers who **settled** the Great Plains **built** their houses of sod.

How would you feel about living in a house literally made of **earth**? Pioneer children on the **prairie** may have found it **exciting**. After all, just when **bordom** was at its worst, something totally **unexpected** might happen. A rodent or a snake could **drop** from the ceiling at any time and **liven** things up rather quickly! What could be **more** exciting than that?

Page 51

Write **F** if the statement a fact and **O** if it is an opinion.

O 1. Abraham Lincoln was a homely man.

O 2. Grace Bedell was a disrespectful little girl.

F 3. Grace Bedell lived in Westfield, New York.

O 4. All ladies in Lincoln's day preferred men with beards.

F 5. Abraham Lincoln did not have a beard before 1860.

F 6. Lincoln had a difficult time growing a beard.

O 7. Beards make men look distinguished.

F 8. Lincoln met Grace Bedell on his way to his inauguration.

Number the following events in the order in which they occurred.

4 Lincoln answers Grace Bedell's letter.

8 Lincoln is inaugurated as President.

7 Lincoln meets Grace Bedell.

2 Grace Bedell's father shows her a picture of Abe Lincoln.

5 Lincoln begins to grow a beard.

3 Grace Bedell suggests to Lincoln that he grow a beard.

6 Lincoln begins his journey to Washington for his inauguration.

1 Lincoln is nominated for the presidency.

Page 53

Write the letter of the correct answer to complete each statement.

b 1. Plato was a famous Greek . . .
(a) ruler. (b) philosopher.
(c) warrior. (d) artist.

d 2. Plato believed the continent of Atlantis was located . . .
(a) in the Mediterranean. (b) near Bermuda.
(c) in the North Sea. (d) in the Atlantic Ocean.

a 3. Plato learned of Atlantis by studying the records of the . . .
(a) ruler Solon. (b) ancient Egyptians.
(c) city of Athens. (d) people of Atlantis themselves.

b 4. Atlantis was believed to have been destroyed by . . .
(a) invading armies. (b) earthquakes and floods.
(c) a volcano. (d) a deadly virus.

a 5. Plato believed the people of Atlantis had brought destruction on themselves because they had . . .
(a) grown greedy. (b) lost interest in their government.
(c) become lazy. (d) disbanded their army.

Page 55

Number the following events in order.

Wilt Chamberlain . . .

6 was traded to the Philadelphia 76ers.

3 became a member of the Philadelphia Warriors.

8 retired from professional basketball.

1 scored 52 points in a game at the University of Kansas.

7 was traded to the Los Angeles Lakers.

2 played for the Harlem Globetrotters.

4 scored 100 points in a game against the New York "Knicks."

5 led the NBA with a 50.4 scoring average.

Answer the following question.

Do you think any player will ever again score 100 points in a professional basketball game? Why or why not? **Opinions will vary.**

Page 57

Fill in the blanks below to complete the statements.

1. The Ghost Dance was practiced on the **Great** Plains.
2. Some Indians thought that ghost **shirts** would protect them from the white man's bullets.
3. **Wovoka** had the vision that led to the introduction of the Ghost Dance.
4. Some Indians believed that a **Messiah** would restore their lands to them.
5. Wounded Knee was a creek in South **Dakota**.
6. Wovoka lived on a reservation in **Nevada**.
7. Wovoka was a member of the **Paiute** tribe.
8. A terrible tragedy occurred at Wounded **Knee** in 1890.
9. Indians who danced the Ghost Dance often fell into a **trance**.
10. A medicine man named **Yellow** Bird was partly responsible for the massacre that occurred at Wounded Knee.

Page 59

Replace the underlined words in the sentences below with words that make each of the sentences a true statement.

1. The Greeks invented myths to <u>amuse themselves</u>.
   explain the world around them
2. Joe Magarac was a <u>real person</u> said to have been born in a <u>steel mill</u>. **mythical hero; ore mountain**
3. Mary Mestrovich <u>hoped Joe Magarac would win the weightlifting contest</u>. **took little interest in the contest**
4. Mary's father said his daughter could marry only <u>Magarac</u>.
   man who proved he was strongest
5. Magarac entered the contest <u>to win the hand of Mary</u>.
   just to win
6. Joe Magarac <u>looked forward to marrying</u> **said he had no time for marriage**

Page 61

Write the main idea of each of the following paragraphs.

Paragraph #2
Immigrant children had to work to help support the family.

Paragraph #4
Boys were hurt and even killed working in the breakers.

Paragraph #5
Boys who worked in the breakers suffered health problems all their lives.

On a separate sheet of paper, answer the questions below.
Answers may vary.
1. How do you think parents felt about apprenticing a son to the mines? **Probably felt they had no choice...**
2. Why do you think the government enacted laws that eventually put an end to children working in such places as mines?

Page 63

Use the Word Bank to complete the sentences.

Word Bank
impressed   place   stealing
blacks   major   toured

1. Most **blacks** who went west were homesteaders.
2. Estimates **place** the number of black cowboys at 5,000.
3. The Fourth of July was a **major** holiday on the western frontier.
4. The citizens of Deadwood were very **impressed** with the cowboy skills of Nat Love.
5. Bill Pickett **toured** the country as a rodeo performer.
6. Isom Dart made a career of **stealing** cows rather than driving them.

Page 65

Circle the word or words in the following sentences that makes them false. Then, write a word(s) that would make each sentence true.

1. The sack race was ~~once~~ an Olympic event. **never**
2. The sack race covered a distance of 100 ~~meters~~. **yards**
3. The sack race is ~~still~~ a track and field event today. **not**
4. The Olympic Games were first held in ancient ~~Rome~~. **Greece**
5. Chariot racing was a ~~safe~~ sport. **dangerous**
6. The pankration combined boxing with ~~running~~. **wrestling**
7. Johnny Finn was an outstanding ~~sprinter~~. **sack racer**
8. The sack race was once a part of ~~all~~ track and field meets. **some.**
9. Participants in a sack race hopped along in ~~paper bags~~. **burlap sacks (bags)**
10. It took Johnny Finn only ~~six~~ seconds longer than a sprinter to cover a distance of 100 yards. **four**

Page 67

Use the words from the Word Bank to fill in the blanks.

Word Bank			
business	delivering	history	most	smoked
carried	fired	large	name	worked
customer	freight	later	remember	famous

Mary Fields is one of the **most** interesting characters in the **history** of the Old West. She was a **large** woman who stood six feet tall. She **carried** a gun and often **smoked** a cigar.

Mary got her **name** "Stagecoach" when she started **delivering** mail in Cascade, Montana. But first she **worked** at a Catholic mission. After hauling **freight** at the mission for ten years, she was **fired** by the bishop.

Mary went into the restaurant **business** for awhile but was not successful. In her **later** years, she ran a laundry in Cascade. Townsfolk **remember** her for punching out a **customer** who refused to pay his bill.

Gary Cooper, who grew up to become a **famous** movie star, knew Mary when he was a child in Cascade.

Thinking Cap: Why do you think characters like Stagecoach Mary are sometimes idolized by the people who know them? Do you think they are deserving of such respect? **Answers will vary.**

Page 69

Underline the meaning that describes each word as used in the story.

1. **stunned** (a) shocked (b) knocked unconscious
2. **upset** (a) disturbed (b) defeat unexpectedly
3. **figure** (a) likeness (b) amount
4. **passed** (a) gone by (b) threw
5. **league** (a) an association of sports teams (b) a measure of distance
6. **bowl** (a) a hollow, rounded dish (b) a football game played after the regular season
7. **coach** (a) a person who trains athletic teams (b) a carriage
8. **completion** (a) a caught forward pass (b) finishing
9. **season** (a) one of the four periods of a year (b) a time when something is occurring
10. **yards** (a) pieces of land near or around a house, school, etc. (b) measured distances on a football field

Page 71

To the left of each statement, write **F** if it is a fragment, or part of a sentence. Write **S** if it is a complete sentence.

F 1. Althea Gibson from Silver, South Carolina.
S 2. The ATA was a tennis association for black players.
F 3. Moved his family to New York.
F 4. Played paddle tennis in the streets.
F 5. Learned tennis quickly.
S 6. The USLTA practiced discrimination against blacks.
S 7. Althea lost at Forest Hills.
F 8. Won the French Open.
S 9. Althea was 5'10" tall.
F 10. ATA women's champion for ten consecutive years.
F 11. Alice Marble, former champion.
S 12. Althea Gibson won a Wimbledon title in her career.

at the startled pilot in the open cockpit. One brick led to another, and the aerial war was on! From bricks the pilots graduated to rusty chains and other objects. Some dangled heavy weights from long wires hoping to entangle the enemy's propeller. Eventually the aviators began firing at each other with pistols, muskets, shotguns, and rifles. When machineguns synchronized to fire through propeller blades became standard on planes, the shooting war began in earnest.

As World War I progressed, pilots on both sides lost their lives in increasing numbers. But in the early days of the war, aerial combat was little more than an amusing sideshow in contrast to the horror that was taking place in the trenches below.

On the blank lines below, replace the underlined words with words that make each sentence a true statement.

1. In the story, the term *dogfight* refers to <u>fights between trained dogs</u>.

_____

2. Most military experts <u>were excited about the future of the airplane in combat</u>.

_____

3. At the start of WWI, the airplane was used only for <u>bombing</u>.

_____

4. <u>Rusty chains</u> were the first *weapons* used by pilots in combat.

_____

5. Machineguns that fired through an airplane's <u>cockpit</u> made air combat deadly. _____

The Ship of the Desert

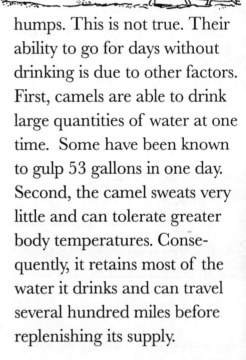

Nomads who crisscross the Sahara Desert of North Africa rely on a most unique animal for transportation—the dromedary, or one-humped camel. The two-humped camel, or the Bactrian camel, is found in Central Asia. Because it is indispensable to desert travel, the dromedary is sometimes called the "ship of the desert."

Several factors make the dromedary suitable for long desert trips. It can go for long periods without nourishment. The hump on a camel's back serves as its food reserve. When it has little to eat, it converts the fat from its hump into energy. The camel's hump can weigh up to 80 pounds or more. When the animal has to rely on its reservoir of fat, the hump becomes much smaller. Thus, it is easy to recognize a well-fed camel by the size of its hump.

Many people believe that camels store water in their humps. This is not true. Their ability to go for days without drinking is due to other factors. First, camels are able to drink large quantities of water at one time. Some have been known to gulp 53 gallons in one day. Second, the camel sweats very little and can tolerate greater body temperatures. Consequently, it retains most of the water it drinks and can travel several hundred miles before replenishing its supply.

Other physical characteristics enable the camel to endure the harsh desert conditions. It can completely close its nostrils, thus protecting it from the stinging effects of sandstorms. Its eyes are shielded from sand and sun by overhanging lids and long lashes, and its broad, padded feet keep it from sinking into the soft sand. No other animal is better equipped for life in the desert than the camel.

Camels serve the nomadic peoples of North Africa in many ways. First, because they are tall, strong animals, capable of carrying loads up to a thousand pounds, the nomads use them for transportation and portage. Second, their long hair is used to weave the cloth from which tents are made. Third, their milk and meat are often part of the nomads' diet. Finally, camels can sniff out water holes from miles away!

Answer the questions below.

1. What is the main idea expressed in the story?

_____

2. How are the dromedary and the Bactrian camel different?

_____

_____

3. What is the purpose of the camel's hump?

_____

4. List the physical characteristics that make the camel suitable for desert travel? _____

_____

_____

5. Name three ways in which the camel is useful to desert people.

_____

_____

_____

A True Hero

Roberto Clemente was one of the greatest baseball players of all time. In 18 seasons with the Pittsburgh Pirates of the National League, he recorded 3,000 base hits and had a lifetime batting average of .317. In 1960 and in 1971, he led his team to both the National League and the World Series championships. Four times he topped the National League in batting. He was a baseball hero both teammates and opponents admired.

But Clemente was a hero in an even more important way. In December of 1972, a series of earthquakes rocked the city of Managua in the Central American nation of Nicaragua. At least 10,000 people were killed in the worst disaster to strike the Western Hemisphere in many years. In San Juan, Puerto Rico, a well-known television personality appealed to his fellow Puerto Ricans to help the suffering people of Nicaragua. He asked Clemente, a native Puerto Rican, to help him raise emergency supplies to be flown to the stricken area.

Clemente appeared on San Juan television and appealed to the people of Puerto Rico. The response was tremendous. The people of San Juan came in droves with their donations. They brought food, clothes, blankets, and medical supplies. Within two days, the first relief planes took off for Nicaragua.

As is often the case in disasters, some of the relief supplies flown to Nicaragua began to fall into the wrong hands. Donations confiscated by black marketeers never got through to the people who needed them. To prevent this, Clemente decided to fly to Nicaragua himself. It was a decision that cost him his life.

At 9 P.M. on New Year's Eve, 1972, an old DC-7 carrying Clemente and others with a load of supplies took off from San Juan. Ninety seconds later, its pilot radioed the tower that he was turning back. Something had apparently gone wrong, but the pilot did not elaborate and said nothing else. The DC-7 crashed off the Puerto Rican coast, killing Clemente and the others.

When they heard the news, thousands of Puerto Ricans made their way to the coast. They waited three days for news of Clemente. After some time, only the body of the pilot was found, along with pieces of the cockpit.

Write **F** if you think the statement is a fact and **O** if it is an opinion.

_____ 1. Clemente was the greatest player in the history of baseball.

_____ 2. Clemente had a lifetime batting average of over .300.

_____ 3. Had it not been for Clemente, the Pittsburgh Pirates might never have won a National League championship.

_____ 4. Roberto Clemente was the greatest hitter of all time.

_____ 5. Clemente helped the Pirates win two World Series championships.

_____ 6. Had he not died in a tragic accident, Roberto Clemente would have set even more records in baseball.

_____ 7. Clemente played his entire major league career with the Pittsburgh Pirates.

_____ 8. Clemente appealed to the people of Puerto Rico to help the victims of the Nicaraguan earthquake.

_____ 9. All Puerto Ricans loved and respected Roberto Clemente.

_____ 10. Pilot error probably caused the crash of the DC-7 that killed Clemente and others.

One Stubborn Italian!

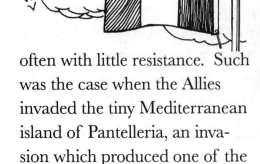

Unlike most of their German counterparts, the majority of Italians had little stomach for World War II. Forced into the conflict by dictator Benito Mussolini in 1940, they were happy when Italy signed an armistice in September 1943. Their German allies, however, were not quite so ecstatic and occupied Italy within hours after the Italians quit the fight.

Although some Italians fought with enthusiam, most did not. Many felt a certain kinship with the United States and its allies. Thousands of Italians had emigrated to America starting in the late 1800s, and many of their relatives still lived in Italy. There was also a large number of Italians who had lived in the United States before the war and who greeted American soldiers as long-lost friends.

As the fortunes of war turned against Italy, Italian soldiers began to surrender in droves, often with little resistance. Such was the case when the Allies invaded the tiny Mediterranean island of Pantelleria, an invasion which produced one of the war's more humorous incidents.

Since Pantelleria blocked the way to Sicily, it had to be taken before the larger island could be assaulted. Beginning in May 1943, Allied planes and ships bombarded Pantelleria daily. The day before the invasion, so many bombers were in the air over the tiny island simultaneously that some had to hold in a circling pattern and wait their turn. After five weeks, the Allies considered the Italians sufficiently softened up, and on June 11, a small British force came ashore.

The 11,000 dazed and shell-shocked Italians defending the island gave up without firing a shot. One of the island's inhabitants, however, did not concede quite so easily. As a result, there *was* an Allied casualty. A not-so-vigilant British soldier was bitten by a local donkey! The soldier survived. We can only assume that the donkey did also.

Write the letter of the correct answer to complete each statement.

___ 1. Benito Mussolini was the . . .
   (a) dictator of Italy.
   (b) prime minister of Great Britain.
   (c) leader of Nazi Germany.
   (d) Italian commander at Pantelleria.

___ 2. The majority of Italians . . .
   (a) supported the war.
   (b) were happy to get out of the war.
   (c) were zealous fighters.
   (d) had no opinion about the war.

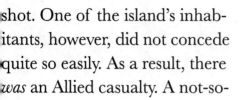

___ 3. Pantelleria was . . .
   (a) a small city near Rome.
   (b) a city on the island of Sicily.
   (c) an island in the Atlantic.
   (d) an island in the Mediterranean.

___ 4. The Allies had to take Pantelleria before invading . . .
   (a) Italy.   (b) France.
   (c) Sicily.   (d) Germany.

___ 5. The British who invaded Pantelleria suffered . . .
   (a) many casualties   (b) not a single casualty
   (c) 11,000 casualties   (d) one casualty (of a sort)

Ant Ambushers

Ants can be a problem. They sting, they invade our homes, and they can make shambles of a perfect picnic.

But ants have problems, too, especially those ants that live in sandy places such as dunes and deserts. Not the least of their problems are the larvae of two insects that ambush their prey from concealed sand traps. One of these insects is the tiger beetle. The other is the ant lion.

To escape the intense heat at the sand's surface, the tiger beetle larva digs a vertical tunnel up to two feet deep. There it remains until it is hungry. When mealtime approaches, the larva lurks near the rim of its burrow, clinging to the sides by two large hooks protruding from a hump on its back. All the time it plugs the opening to the tunnel with its enormous head. When an unsuspecting prey approaches, the larva springs out in a somersault motion and grabs the victim with its massive, sword-like jaws and pulls it into the tunnel. If, by chance, the larva itself is ever in danger of becoming a meal for some larger predator, it uses its hooks to dig into the sides of its trap.

The ant lion larva uses an even cleverer device to snare its prey. And it expends much less energy. It digs a cone-shaped tunnel, which it covers at the top with a layer of sand. Then it waits at the bottom of the pit with its large jaws open. When an ant or other insect ventures across the trap, the sand at the top collapses and the ant lion's meal tumbles down to be injected with a paralyzing poison by the ant lion. If the trapped insect manages to cling to the rim at the top, the ant lion can flip additional sand to the surface. This action usually causes the victim to lose its grip so it comes tumbling back down the tunnel to be poisoned and devoured.

At maturity, the life spans of the tiger beetle and the ant lion vary considerably. The former lives on as a beetle and contin-ues its ravenous ways on the surface of the sand. But the latter changes from its squat larva stage to become an attractive insect resembling a damselfly. It then flies off and lives only long enough to mate and lay its eggs.

Complete the Venn diagram with facts about tiger beetle and ant lion larvae. Write characteristics common to both where the circles overlap.

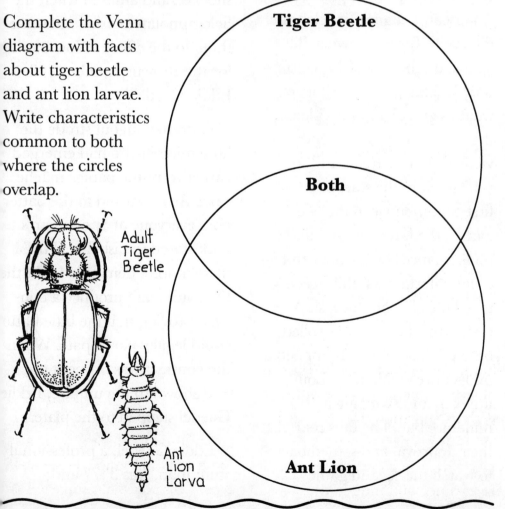

Adult
Tiger
Beetle

Tiger Beetle

Both

Ant
Lion
Larva

Ant Lion

The Littlest Major Leaguer

The date was August 19, 1951. The place was Sportsman's Park in St. Louis. The occasion was a double-header between the St. Louis Browns and the Detroit Tigers.

The year marked the fiftieth anniversary of baseball's American League. To celebrate the event, Browns' owner Bill Veeck, on the day of his club's doubleheader with the Tigers, went to great lengths to please the crowd. Those in attendance were given free treats and souvenirs before the start of the first game. Between the two games, the fans were treated to performances by jugglers and other entertainers. Bill Veeck saved the clincher for last. A papier-mâché cake was rolled onto the field, and out popped a midget dressed in a St. Louis uniform and swinging a minature bat. The fans roared their approval and settled back to watch the second game.

But Bill Veeck had not run out of surprises. In the very first inning of the second game, a pinch hitter was announced for a Brown batter. The crowd was shocked and amused when the field announcer cried out something to the effect: "Now batting for the Browns, number 1/8, Eddie Gaedel."

From the dugout strode the little midget who had emerged earlier from the papier-mâché cake. As he walked to the batter' box, everyone at Sportsman's Park stared in disbelief. The plate umpire demanded that the St. Louis team produce a contract proving that the little batter could legally participate. When the contract was brought out and shown to the umpire, Eddie Gaedel stepped to the plate.

Eddie Gaedel, a professional stunt man, was 3' 7" and

weighed 65 pounds. Bill Veeck had signed him to a one-day contract with instructions not to swing. He was told to crouch as low as possible and draw a walk from the Detroit pitcher. No matter how hard the opposing hurler tried, he could not throw a single ball in the strike zone. Little Eddie Gaedel walked, and sauntered proudly down to first base. Immediately he was replaced by a pinch runner, and his major league career was over.

Answer the questions below.

1. What event was being celebrated on the day Eddie Gaedel appeared in a major league game? _____

2. What was Sportsman's Park? _____

3. Who were the Browns' opponents in the doubleheader?

   _____

4. What was Eddie told not to do when he stepped up to the plate?

   _____

5. In your opinion, was it fair or ethical for Browns' owner Bill Veeck to use Eddie in such a way? Was it degrading for Eddie?

   _____

   _____

   _____

6. If you had been Eddie Gaedel, would you have accepted Bill Veeck's invitation to become a part of the entertainment that day? Why or why not? _____

   _____

Sod Houses

If you had lived on the Great Plains in the late 1800s, you would probably not have resided in a house made of brick, or wood, or even clay. Each of these resources was almost nonexistent on the treeless prairie. Early settlers had to rely on the only building material available to them: sod.

Sod, of course, is nothing more than grass, dirt, and roots. But the sod of the Great Plains is different from that found in other regions. Its roots are thicker and the hot sun bakes it as hard as brick. Settlers plowed and cut it into blocks about 2 to 3 feet long, 1 to 1$\frac{1}{2}$ feet wide, and 4 to 6 inches deep. These blocks were stacked one upon the other like bricks to form the walls of the house, with openings for windows and a door. If the farmer had means, he bought his door and windows in the nearest town or ordered them through the mail. If the farm family was poor, as most were, they fashioned doors and windows from box crates. The roof of the house was also made of sod placed across branches.

Sod houses proved to be comfortable and sturdy. They were warm in winter and cool in summer. They were fireproof, windproof, and, for the most part, bulletproof. Most were buil so strong that they could withstand tornadoes and snowstorms They could also be eye-appealing. When the spring rains came prairie roses and morning glorie sprang from the roof and walls. Sometimes, the wife of the hous added to the colorful array by planting on the roof seeds that she had brought with her along the trail.

But sod houses had their draw backs, too. They were dark,

damp, smoky, and smelly. During heavy rains, the roof leaked, and water and mud often dripped into whatever happened to be cooking on the stove at the time. Worse, insects, rats, and snakes sometimes dropped from the roof and created no small amount of havoc among the family members. There are even cases of cows plummeting through the roofs of early sod houses that were built into the sides of bluffs. Bet you never had a cow drop in for dinner!

Be it ever so humble, the "soddy," as the sod house was affectionately called, was home to most of those hardy souls who braved life on the Great Plains.

Use the words from the Word Bank to fill in the blanks below..

Word Bank

boredom	earth	materials	scarce
built	exciting	more	settled
drop	liven	prairie	unexpected

Because other _____ were _____,
pioneers who _____ the Great Plains _____
their houses of sod.

How would you feel about living in a house literally made of
_____? Pioneer children on the _____ may have
found it _____. After all, just when _____
was at its worst, something totally _____ might
happen. A rodent or a snake could _____ from the ceiling
at any time and _____ things up rather quickly! What could
be _____ exciting than that?

How Mr. Lincoln Got His Beard

Most pictures of Abraham Lincoln that appear in textbooks show him with a beard. But for most of his political life, Lincoln was clean-shaven. It was not until he ran for the presidency in 1860 that he began to grow the beard.

The idea for the beard came from a most unusual source: an 11-year-old girl in Westfield, New York, named Grace Bedell. One day, young Grace's father showed her a picture of Lincoln that he had brought home from a fair. Grace took one look and decided that the future president would look much better with facial hair. His face, she pointed out, was much too thin to be appealing.

Little Grace sat down and immediately penned a letter to the presidential candidate. After listing reasons why she thought a beard would improve Mr. Lincoln's looks, she went on to say that she had four big brothers and that all of them would probably vote for him if he let his whiskers grow. She also added that her father and others would cast their ballot in the same manner. She closed by saying that all the ladies liked beards and that they would pressure their husbands into voting for him too.

Lincoln answered Grace's letter after only four days. He thanked her for her suggestion but stated that since he had not had a beard at any point in his life, people might think him silly if he grew one now. But, two weeks later, having apparently thought it over, he appeared unshaven in public for the first time. His stubble was slow to grow. After two months, it remained scraggly and spotty. It was not until his inauguration hat the beard fully covered his ace. On the way to his inaugu- ration, Lincoln made a point to meet his 11-year-old consultant.

Write **F** if the statement a fact and **O** if it is an opinion.

_____ 1. Abraham Lincoln was a homely man.

_____ 2. Grace Bedell was a disrespectful little girl.

_____ 3. Grace Bedell lived in Westfield, New York.

_____ 4. All ladies in Lincoln's day preferred men with beards.

_____ 5. Abraham Lincoln did not have a beard before 1860.

_____ 6. Lincoln had a difficult time growing a beard.

_____ 7. Beards make men look distinguished.

_____ 8. Lincoln met Grace Bedell on his way to his inauguration.

Number the following events in the order in which they occurred.

_____ Lincoln answers Grace Bedell's letter.

_____ Lincoln is inaugurated as president.

_____ Lincoln meets Grace Bedell.

_____ Grace Bedell's father shows her a picture of Abe Lincoln.

_____ Lincoln begins to grow a beard.

_____ Grace Bedell suggests to Lincoln that he grow a beard.

_____ Lincoln begins his journey to Washington for his inauguration.

_____ Lincoln is nominated for the presidency.

Atlantis: Real or Imagined?

Around the year 370 B.C., the Greek philosopher Plato wrote about a huge continent that once existed in the Atlantic Ocean. Plato called the continent "Atlantis" and stated that it was approximately the size of Europe. It was the home of a mighty nation with powerful armies that had subdued parts of Europe and North Africa. Plato even wrote that its armies had once attacked Athens but that they were beaten back.

Plato's account of Atlantis came from researching the records of an earlier Athenian ruler named Solon. Solon was supposed to have visited Egypt several hundred years before, and it was there that he heard about Atlantis.

Atlantis was said to have beautiful cities with advanced technologies. The climate was so ideal that two growing seasons were possible. The continent teemed with herbs, fruits, and plants and was the habitat of many animals, including elephants. Life was good until, according to Plato, the citizens of Atlantis became greedy and incurred the wrath of the gods. Then great earthquakes and floods that continued nonstop for a day and a night caused the continent to sink into the ocean.

Fact or fiction? No evidence has been produced to prove that Atlantis ever existed. Some scholars think Plato may have even made the story up. Other writers support the idea that Atlantis was real, but they place the continent in a different locale. One, Edgar Cayce, believed Atlantis was near the Bermuda Island of Bimini. He wrote that its people were so advanced that they had "fire crystals," or power towers, with which they harnassed energy.

Cayce also believed that some catastrophic occurrence caused the continent to sink. He goes further to state that the fire crystals might be an explanation for the so-called Bermuda Triangle, an area that is said to be responsible for the disappearance of numerous ships and airplanes in the waters bordering Bermuda, Puerto Rico, and Ft. Lauderdale, Florida. Cayce believed that the fire crystals that sank with the continent send out an energy field that pulls ships and planes toward it.

What do you think? Far-fetched or possible?

Write the letter of the correct answer to complete each statement.

_____ 1. Plato was a famous Greek . . .
(a) ruler.
(b) philosopher.
(c) warrior.
(d) artist.

_____ 2. Plato believed the continent of Atlantis was located . . .
(a) in the Mediterranean.
(b) near Bermuda.
(c) in the North Sea.
(d) in the Atlantic Ocean.

_____ 3. Plato learned of Atlantis by studying the records of the . . .
(a) ruler Solon.
(b) ancient Egyptians.
(c) city of Athens.
(d) people of Atlantis themselves.

_____ 4. Atlantis was believed to have been destroyed by . . .
(a) invading armies.
(b) earthquakes and floods.
(c) a volcano.
(d) a deadly virus.

_____ 5. Plato believed the people of Atlantis had brought destruction on themselves because they had . . .
(a) grown greedy.
(b) lost interest in their government.
(c) become lazy.
(d) disbanded their army.

"Wilt the Stilt"

Who was the first professional basketball player to amass more than 30,000 points in his career? Michael Jordan? No.

Who, in one season, averaged 50.4 points a game and scored a total of 4,029 points? Michael Jordan? No, again.

And who is the only professional basketball player to score 100 points in a game? Michael Jordan? No for a third time.

Michael Jordan, to be sure, is perhaps the greatest recent professional basketball player. His shooting ability and acrobatic moves have been admired by all. But the records mentioned above belong to a player who displayed his amazing skills some 30 years before Michael Jordan came on the scene. That player is Wilt Chamberlain.

Wilt Chamberlain joined the NBA (National Basketball Association) after an illustrious career at the University of Kansas. In his very first varsity game at Kansas, the 7'1" Chamberlain scored 52 points. Known as "Wilt the Stilt" because of his height, he played one year with the Harlem Globetrotters before joining the Philadelphia (now Golden State) Warriors in 1959. In 1961–62, he led the league with 4,029 points, a whopping 50.4-point average a game. In 1965 he was traded to the Philadelphia 76ers and in 1968 to the Los Angeles Lakers. He led both of those teams to NBA titles.

One record set by the mighty Wilt may never be broken: that of scoring 100 points in a single game. Wilt accomplished that feat on the night of March 2, 1962, in Hershey, Pennsylvania. His team, the Philadelphia Warriors, played the New York Knickerbockers. Neither team had a shot at making the play-offs, and the game turned into a scoring frenzy. Wilt attempted 63 field goals and hit on 36 of them. At the free throw line, he was 28 out of 32. The game ended with the Warriors winning 169 to 147.

In a 14-year NBA career, Wilt Chamberlain scored 31,419 points. He was the first player ever to exceed the 30,000-point mark. He also grabbed 23,924 rebounds. Would you agree that Wilt Chamberlain was one phenomenal basketball player?

Number the following events in order.

Wilt Chamberlain . . .

____ was traded to the Philadelphia 76ers.

____ became a member of the Philadelphia Warriors.

____ retired from professional basketball.

____ scored 52 points in a game at the University of Kansas.

____ was traded to the Los Angeles Lakers.

____ played for the Harlem Globetrotters.

____ scored 100 points in a game against the New York "Knicks."

____ led the NBA with a 50.4 scoring average.

Answer the following question.

Do you think any player will ever again score 100 points in a professional basketball game? Why or why not? _____

_____

_____

The Ghost Dance

In the late 1880s, the Indians of the Great Plains faced virtual extinction. Their lands had been taken away, and the buffalo, the source of their very existence, had been slaughtered by greedy white hunters. On the brink of starvation, some turned in desperation to what was called the religion of the Ghost Dance.

In 1888, a Paiute Indian on a reservation in Nevada had a vision. During a fever, he dreamed he visited the Great Spirit in the sky. The Great Spirit told him that a Messiah would come to restore the country to the Indians. The earth would be reborn, and, in the process, all white people would be buried under the new soil. The buffalo would return, and the living would be reunited with departed loved ones.

How was this to come about? Wovoka, the Paiute who claimed to have had the vision and who came to be called the "Paiute Messiah," instructed his people to dance the Ghost Dance. He said that the Great Spirit had taught it to him in his vision. While dancing, participants fell into a hypnotic trance and believed they were communicating with the ghosts of the dead. The dance quickly spread to other reservations, causing tension to mount between Indians and whites.

The Ghost Dance in itself was perfectly harmless. At no point did Wovoka and others preach war against the whites. But some Sioux Indians twisted Wovoka's peaceful message into a call to arms. They even started wearing "ghost shirts," which they claimed would prevent bullets from hurting them. The Sioux's interpretation of the Ghost Dance ritual caused the U.S. Seventh Cavalry to believe an uprising was in the making.

Disaster struck shortly after Christmas 1890. A band of Sioux under Chief Big Foot was on its way to the Pine Ridge Agency in South Dakota to turn themselves in. They were intercepted by a troop of cavalry, who decided to disarm the ragged band at a creek named Wounded Knee. A scuffle broke out, and shots were fired. A medicine man named Yellow Bird shouted to the Sioux that their ghost shirts would protect them from army bullets, and some of the Indians charged the soldiers. The result was a massacre. Nearly 200 Indians, including many women and children, were killed.

Fill in the blanks below to complete the statements.

1. The Ghost Dance was practiced on the _____ Plains.

2. Some Indians thought that ghost _____ would protect them from the white man's bullets.

3. _____ had the vision that led to the introduction of the Ghost Dance.

4. Some Indians believed that a _____ would restore their lands to them.

5. Wounded Knee was a creek in South _____.

6. Wovoka lived on a reservation in _____.

7. Wovoka was a member of the _____ tribe.

8. A terrible tragedy occurred at Wounded _____ in 1890.

9. Indians who danced the Ghost Dance often fell into a _____.

10. A medicine man named _____ Bird was partly responsible for the massacre that occurred at Wounded Knee.

Joe Magarac

Since the beginning of time, people have invented mythical stories and mythical characters. The Greeks and other ancient peoples invented myths to explain the world around them. Centuries later and an ocean away, frontiersmen, immigrants, and others who helped build America also created myths.

One such mythical hero was Joe Magarac. Joe Magarac was a seven-foot giant who fashioned steel railroad rails with his bare hands. The Hungarian and Slovakian steelworkers of western Pennsylvania boasted that Joe was born in an ore mountain and was made completely of steel. He was a nineteenth-century Superman.

One Fourth of July, a steelworker named Steve Mestrovich staged a weightlifting contest for the hand of his daughter Mary. He announced that his pretty daughter could wed only the man who proved himself to be the strongest person in the world. As for Mary, she already had a beau and took little interest in the contest. Her headstrong father, however, was determined that only the person who lifted the heaviest weight could become her husband.

Many young men from the surrounding area entered the competition. One after another fell short in his effort and was required to sit with the children in attendance. Along came Joe, who asked to give the weights a try. He had no interest in winning Mary, only in winning the contest. With no effort at all, he lifted a 1,000-pound weight.

Joe Magarac won the competition but forthwith stated that he had no time for marrying. He explained that he worked around the clock, stopping only five times a day to eat a meal of hot steel soup. That suited pretty Mary Mestrovich just

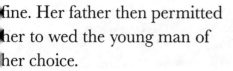

fine. Her father then permitted her to wed the young man of her choice.

Not too long after the contest, Joe melted himself down in a vat of boiling metal. His reason for doing so depends on which story you prefer. One holds that, because the finest steel was needed to build a new mill, and Joe was the finest steel around, he sacrificed himself to the cause. The other maintains that Joe destroyed himself in protest after his mill was shut down. Either way, Joe Magarac, the man of steel, became a hero to steelworkers everywhere.

Replace the underlined words in the sentences below with words that make each of the sentences a true statement.

1. The Greeks invented myths to amuse themselves.

   _____

2. Joe Magarac was a real person said to have been born in a steel mill. _____

3. Mary Mestrovich hoped Joe Magarac would win the weightlifting contest. _____

   _____

4. Mary's father said his daughter could marry only Magarac.

   _____

5. Magarac entered the contest to win the hand of Mary.

   _____

6. Joe Magarac looked forward to marrying. _____

   _____

The Boys in the Breakers

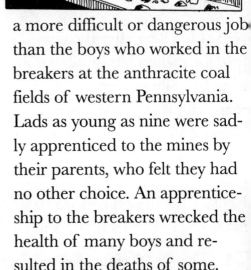

As a sixth-grade student, you are old enough to earn spending money doing various odd jobs. Perhaps you occasionally baby-sit, or care for your neighbor's dog. Maybe you have a paper route. And you may even look forward to the day when you can have a permanent part-time job.

But suppose you were an immigrant who arrived in America more than a hundred years ago. Chances are you would have *had* to work. Your parents would have been so poorly paid that you and your brothers and sisters would have had to work just to help put food on the family table. You probably would not even have gone to school. You would have worked at a back-breaking job for 12 hours a day and been paid a total of 60 cents for your efforts. And there is a good possibility that your job would have been dangerous.

No immigrant child ever had a more difficult or dangerous job than the boys who worked in the breakers at the anthracite coal fields of western Pennsylvania. Lads as young as nine were sadly apprenticed to the mines by their parents, who felt they had no other choice. An apprenticeship to the breakers wrecked the health of many boys and resulted in the deaths of some.

A breaker was a tall building where lumps of coal were broken into smaller sizes before being cleaned and washed. On the way to the washer, pieces of slate had to be hand-picked from the pieces of coal. This was the job of the boys who worked in the breaker. From sunrise to sunset, young boys leaned over the chutes, removing the slate as the coal passed by. Since anthracite coal is very hard, fingers were constantly bruised or crushed. Sometimes hands got caught and mangled in the machinery that moved the chutes. And sometimes boys who were tired and not alert were even pulled into the chutes to be crushed and suffocated by the coal and dust.

Boys who survived the breakers were marked for life. Many became permanently stooped from leaning over the chutes for long periods of time. Others developed asthma or tuberculosis from years of breathing coal dust. Fortunately, laws were later enacted that abolished these and other abuses associated with child labor.

Write the main idea of each of the following paragraphs.

Paragraph #2

_____

_____

Paragraph #4

_____

_____

Paragraph #5

_____

_____

On a separate sheet of paper, answer the questions below.

1. How do you think parents felt about apprenticing a son to the mines?

2. Why do you think the government enacted laws that eventually put an end to children working in such places as mines?

Black Cowboys

The years following the Civil War were difficult ones for newly freed slaves in the South. In spite of constitutional amendments granting them citizenship and voting rights, blacks remained, as before, subject to prejudice, discrimination, and acts of terrorism. Seeing no future for themselves in the ex-Confederacy, many former slaves struck out for the West in hopes of finding a better life.

Most blacks who migrated west became homesteaders on the Great Plains. But there were also missionaries, soldiers, journalists, forty-niners, pony express riders, a few outlaws, and cowboys aplenty. Until the railroads put an end to cattle drives, more than 5,000 black cowboys helped herd Texas Longhorns up the Chisholm Trail from Texas to Kansas and other points north. Most were hard workers who gained the respect of the whites with whom they worked. On the trail, they were usually treated as equals and received the same pay as other cowboys. Some displayed such exceptional skills as marksmen, ropers, and riders that they became famous throughout the West.

One famous black cowboy was Nat Love. Love went west at the age of 15 and became a trail hand for $30 a month. In 1876, he arrived in Deadwood on July 4, in time for the annual Independence Day celebration, a major holiday throughout the Western frontier. Love entered the roping and shooting contests and easily defeated his white counterparts. The citizens of Deadwood were so impressed with his skills that they gave him the nickname "Deadwood Dick" and proclaimed him the best roper in the territory.

Alas, like some white trail hands, a few black cowboys ran

afoul of the law. One was Isom Dart, who became a cattle rustler. Dart was a likeable sort who never shot anyone and made numerous efforts to go "straight." Whether he would have succeeded is uncertain, for in 1900 he was killed by a white bounty hunter.

Perhaps the best-known black cowboy was Bill Pickett. Pickett was so talented at cowboy skills that he became a rodeo performer and toured the country with a wild west show. Bill Pickett is credited with inventing the rodeo event called "bulldogging," or steer wrestling. In bulldogging, a rider leaps from a galloping horse, grabs a running steer by the horns, and wrestles it to the ground.

Use the Word Bank to complete the sentences.

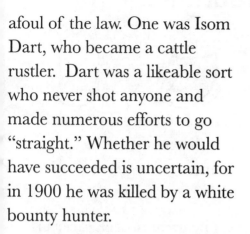

Word Bank		
impressed	place	stealing
blacks	major	toured

1. Most _____ who went west were homesteaders.

2. Estimates _____ the number of black cowboys at 5,000.

3. The Fourth of July was a _____ holiday on the western frontier.

4. The citizens of Deadwood were very _____ with the cowboy skills of Nat Love.

5. Bill Pickett _____ the country as a rodeo performer.

6. Isom Dart made a career of _____ cows rather than driving them.

Championship Sack Racing?

You are sitting in front of your television watching the results of a track and field meet. You are only half-interested as the announcer informs you who won the various races and who placed first in the pole vault and shot put. Then, just as you are about to fall asleep and spill your bag of chips, you are jolted to attention when the news-caster announces the winner of the sack race.

Sack race? "Surely you jest," you say to yourself. Sack races are common occurrences at picnics and school functions, but in a track and field meet? Get serious!

Sack races, to be sure, are not a part of meets today. But in the early twentiethth century, the sack race was an important event in some track and field competitions. Racers participating in the event crawled into a burlap sack and "hopped" their way along a track. Spectators may have found the event amusing, but the athletes bouncing along in the sacks took it seriously.

The greatest sack racer in history was said to have been Johnny Finn of Brooklyn, New York. Finn set a world record in 1929 when he won the 100-yard sack race with a time of 14.4 seconds. To put that mark in the proper perspective, the sprinter who won the 100-yard dash in the same meet was credited with a time of 10.4 seconds. It took Johnny Finn, shuffling along in a burlap sack, only four seconds longer to go the same distance.

It is not unusual for competitive events such as the sack race to come and go. This is true even of the Olympic Games. A popular event of the early Olympics in Greece that was eventually discontinued was the chariot race. So many charioteers were maimed or killed in accidents that the sport was dropped from competition.

Another event of the early Olympics was the pankration. It was a combination of boxing and wrestling in which anything except biting and gouging was permitted. Participants were even allowed to jump up and down on each other's chest. It too resulted in many deaths and was phased out of the games.

Circle the word or words in the following sentences that makes them false. Then, write a word(s) that would make each sentence true.

1. The sack race was once an Olympic event. _____

2. The sack race covered a distance of 100 meters. _____

3. The sack race is still a track and field event today. _____

4. The Olympic Games were first held in ancient Rome.

   _____

5. Chariot racing was a safe sport. _____

6. The pankration combined boxing with running. _____

7. Johnny Finn was an outstanding sprinter. _____

8. The sack race was once a part of all track and field meets.

   _____

9. Participants in a sack race hopped along in paper bags.

   _____

10. It took Johnny Finn only six seconds longer than a sprinter to cover a distance of 100 yards. _____

Stagecoach Mary

Few histories mention that there were black women who made names for themselves on the Western frontier. One of the most interesting is Mary Fields, known throughout Montana in the 1880s as Stagecoach Mary.

Mary Fields was an ex-slave from Tennessee who showed up in the small Montana town of Cascade in 1884. At six feet tall and two hundred pounds, she was an imposing sight. Towns-folk said she could hold her own against any man around. In spite of her rough manner and the fact that she carried a gun under her apron, people liked her and were attracted to her. Actor Gary Cooper knew her when he was a child in Cascade and was captivated by every-thing she did.

Mary's first job was at St. Peter's Catholic Mission in Cascade. She worked there for ten years, hauling freight and doing heavy work for the nuns.

Her time at the mission ended, however, when she and a hired hand got into a gunfight. No one was injured, but the bishop in charge fired her immediately.

With the help of the Mother Superior at the mission, Mary opened a restaurant in Cascade. She failed miserably, apparently having no head for business. Next, she got a job driving the mail coach between the mission and Cascade. That is how she came to be known as "Stage-coach Mary." She carried the mail for eight years, and neither bad weather nor rough terrain ever kept her from getting the letters through. Gary Cooper remembered her sitting on top of the mail coach dressed in men's clothing and smoking a big cigar. She was in her sixties.

After leaving the mail job, Mary opened a laundry in Cascade. Although she was now n her seventies, she was still as ough as ever. Once a male ustomer refused to pay a $2 aundry bill. Mary saw him in a aloon one day and chased him down. When he turned around, she knocked him out with a single blow. She remains to this day one of the Old West's most fascinating characters.

Use the words from the Word Bank to fill in the blanks.

Word Bank

business	delivering	history	most	smoked
carried	fired	large	name	worked
customer	freight	later	remember	famous

Mary Fields is one of the _____ interesting characters in the _____ of the Old West. She was a _____ woman who stood six feet tall. She _____ a gun and often _____ a cigar.

Mary got her _____ "Stagecoach" when she started _____ mail in Cascade, Montana. But first she _____ at a Catholic mission. After hauling _____ t the mission for ten years, she was _____ by the bishop.

Mary went into the restaurant _____ for a while ut was not successful. In her _____ years, she ran a laundry in Cascade. Townsfolk _____ her for punching out _____ who refused to pay his bill.

Gary Cooper, who grew up to become a _____ movie tar, knew Mary when he was a child in Cascade.

Thinking Cap: Why do you think characters like Stagecoach Mary re sometimes idolized by the people who know them? Do you think hey are deserving of such respect?

Broadway Joe

In January of 1969, the New York Jets stunned the football world by upsetting the Baltimore Colts 16–7 in Super Bowl III. What made the win so dramatic was that quarterback Joe Namath had predicted it.

In the later 1960s, there were two professional football leagues. The older and more established NFL (National Football League) had easily won the first two Super Bowls. The other, the AFL (American Football League), was still considered an upstart by many football followers. Like the Kansas City Chiefs and the Oakland Raiders who represented the AFL in Super Bowls I and II, the New York Jets were expected to go down to an embarrassing defeat. But the Jets won, and their victory eventually led to the two football leagues combining.

One can only guess how great a player Joe Namath might have become had he been completely healthy. Throughout his college and professional careers, he was constantly hampered by knee problems. Paul "Bear" Bryant, his coach at the University of Alabama, called him the greatest player he had ever coached—and this while performing on tw gimpy knees.

In 1965, Joe Namath received $400,000 for signing with the Jets. This was an astronomical figure for that time. His signing proved that the AFL could compete financially with the NFL, and the results soon showed on the playing field. Four years afte becoming a pro, Namath led his team to the historic Super Bowl win over the Colts.

In 12 years as a professional, Namath passed for 27,663 yards and 173 touchdowns. He becam the first pro quarterback to thro or 4,000 yards in a season, accomplishing this feat in 1967. In 1985, he was inducted into Pro Football's Hall of Fame.

Namath was given the name "Broadway Joe" because of his flair for flashy clothes and his love of a good time. But the media blew his party image way out of proportion, and it sometimes overshadowed his accomplishments on the playing field. Namath was a great athlete, and he more than proved it by his statistics as a quarterback and through his leadership on the field. When he retired in 1977, he became a television sports commentator and actor.

Underline the meaning that describes each word as used in the story.

1. **stunned** (a) shocked (b) knocked unconscious

2. **upset** (a) disturbed (b) defeat unexpectedly

3. **figure** (a) likeness (b) amount

4. **passed** (a) gone by (b) threw

5. **league** (a) an association of sports teams (b) a measure of distance

6. **bowl** (a) a hollow, rounded dish (b) a football game played after the regular season

7. **coach** (a) a person who trains athletic teams (b) a carriage

8. **completion** (a) a caught forward pass (b) finishing

9. **season** (a) one of the four periods of a year (b) a time when something is occurring

10. **yards** (a) pieces of land near or around a house, school, etc. (b) measured distances on a football field

Althea Gibson: Tennis Trailblazer

In 1950, Althea Gibson did for tennis what Jackie Robinson had done for major league baseball three years earlier: break the color barrier. She became the first African American—male or female—to play in a major tennis championship in the United States. When she took the court at Forest Hills, New York, she was blazing a trail that other black athletes would later follow. Althea lost in the second round of that event, but the course had been set. By 1958, she had won such prestigious events as the French Open, Wimbledon, and the U.S. singles title.

Althea was born in Silver, South Carolina, in 1927. Her father was a sharecropper who moved his family to New York during the Great Depression. There, Althea began to play paddle tennis in the streets. With the help of the supervisor of the Police Athletic League, which sponsored paddle tennis competition, she also learned to play lawn tennis, as amateur tennis was called at that time.

Althea mastered the game of tennis in quick fashion. Her rangy, 5'10" frame gave her a decided advantage over many of her opponents. At the age of 18, she was good enough to begin competing in the ladies' division of the ATA. The ATA (American Tennis Association), was the league reserved for black tennis players. Blacks were not allowed to compete in events held by the all-white USLTA (United States Lawn Tennis Association).

For ten consecutive years, Althea Gibson was the undisputed women's ATA champion. During much of that time, she was barred from entering major tennis tournaments because of her race. The barrier was finally broken in 1950, thanks in part to a magazine editorial written by a former ladies' champion, Alice Marble. Ms. Marble wrote a lengthy letter to *American Lawn Tennis* criticizing racial discrimination in tennis. She further stated that if Althea were denied the opportunity to play in USLTA national tournaments, that she (Ms. Marble) would be bitterly ashamed of the game to which she had devoted her life.

Alice Marble's letter had the desired effect. Althea Gibson was invited to play in the U.S. National Championships. Though she lost that particular championship, she won the right for great tennis players to compete at the national level regardless of race.

To the left of each statement, write **F** if it is a fragment, or part of a sentence. Write **S** if it is a complete sentence.

____ 1. Althea Gibson from Silver, South Carolina.

____ 2. The ATA was a tennis association for black players.

____ 3. Moved his family to New York.

____ 4. Played paddle tennis in the streets.

____ 5. Learned tennis quickly.

____ 6. The USLTA practiced discrimination against blacks.

____ 7. Althea lost at Forest Hills.

____ 8. Won the French Open.

____ 9. Althea was 5'10" tall.

____10. ATA women's champion for ten consecutive years.

____11. Alice Marble, former champion.

____12. Althea Gibson won a Wimbledon title in her career.

Becoming a Better Reader

There are a number of ways in which you can improve your reading skills and become a better reader. Here are some suggestions.

- **Avoid materials too far below your reading level.** Challenge yourself. Try reading something that may be a grade level higher than what you are accustomed to reading. But be careful; don't try to read material that is *too* difficult.

- **Look up unfamiliar words in a dictionary.** You cannot fully understand any passage you read if you skim over unfamiliar words. Look them up!

- **Watch for context clues.** Often the words preceding and coming after a word will give you a clue to its meaning.

- **Become familiar with prefixes and suffixes.** Prefixes such as "re," "pre," and "un," and suffixes such as "er," "ing," and "ment" are added to base or root words to form many other words. Knowing prefixes and suffixes will increase your reading vocabulary many times over.

- **Ask for help.** Ask your teacher, parent, guardian, or a friend to explain a word or phrase in a passage you do not understand. Don't be shy. Ask for help.